A GUIDE TO WRITING YOUR FIRST NOVEL

A.J. Flowers

ISBN-13: 978-1532712784

ISBN-10: 1532712782

This guide is dedicated to Carly Marino, who has been the most supportive critique partner I could ever ask for.

TABLE OF CONTENTS

Introduction

Welcome to "A Guide to Writing Your First Novel!" I am your host, A.J. Flowers. This is a compilation of everything I've learned over the past few years in writing. This guide encompasses all you'll need to know for how to get started with your first novel, or improve your current one, and is designed to keep you from making the same mistakes many aspiring writers encounter along the way.

What to expect:

Resources You Need

This is not just a guide, but a resource guide. The biggest time-sink when first starting out is getting the right advice. I've compiled all the basic writing rules here and supplemental resources to support them. If you're just starting out, there's a lot of studying you need to catch up on. I'll help you cut through the fat and get to the good stuff.

Mistakes to Avoid!

Hindsight is 20/20. I'll save you months, if not years, by helping you to quickly fix mistakes that'll get your work thrown in the rejection pile. Don't just take my word for it, listen to other authors whose interviews are in this guide. They tell what worked for them and what they would have done differently when they had first started writing.

Marketing Insight & Agent/Publisher Interests

There's a large list of winning pitches from Twitter Pitch Contests at the end of this book. The most important skill you need to develop as a writer trying to sell published work is making a killer pitch. Don't ignore this section just because it's a lot to digest! You don't have to have a Twitter account to benefit, but if you don't, you're missing out on a great writers' community.

How to Use this Guide:
Some of the writing rules listed in this guide may seem rudimentary. (It is a guide for beginners, after all.) However, even if something seems simple, I want you to go along with it anyway. I guarantee many of the writing rules you already know you *also* may feel don't apply to you. (How do I know? Because that was me!) The only time you can break rules is after you've already followed them. Very few debut novels are praised for their literary genius by not following a three act structure or having awkward "stylistic" prose. Try following the rules first, and once you're a big deal, break them to your heart's content.

The best bit of advice I can give is to stay humble, keep an open mind, and always be willing to challenge your work. Just by seeking help from others is a great first step, and I'm here to guide you on what you can not only learn from me, but the other giants in this industry. Throughout this guide you will find linked resources that will include blog posts, Twitter feeds, magazine articles, and Amazon books. And as always, feel free to reach out to me personally. I'm here to help!

WRITING YOUR NOVEL

- MINDSET

- PLOT STRUCTURE

- IN THE BEGINNING...

- CHARACTER DEVELOPMENT

- WORLD-BUILDLING

- PROSE, EDITING, & WRITING STYLE

CHAPTER ONE

Mindset

Who Are You Writing For?

All right, let's get started! You may have already written a draft, or are considering writing one. No matter which boat you're in, you need to have the right mindset to accomplish your goals. First of all, let's decide if your goal to write a super great (but belongs under your pillow) dream journal, or a publishable novel.

Have you considered *who* will read your book? Let me rephrase that: Who will *want* to read your book? Probably not. If you've already written your first book, you likely took the first few years to get through the grueling draft you believed would never end. Then end it did, and you couldn't have been more thrilled! What did you do next? If you're like most first-timers, you think the hard part's over and you're ready to be published. But that's not how it works. The editing and revising process should take twice or even three times as long as it did to even write the first draft!

For now, let's back up and get our heads screwed on straight. The million-dollar question is "Who is your audience?"

Those of you not quite following me yet, allow me to give an example.

John is twenty-one, handsome, graduating from college and ready to end his "single" status. So, John decides to go on a blind date with a girl named Emily.

John is a simple guy and fully believes that if he meets the right girl, she's going to "love me for me." So, on his first date, he doesn't wear anything special. He shows up in his favorite 90's Tee with an old stain on the side.

He meets a nice girl, but doesn't ask about her background, instead he just talks about himself. He has a great time, they order burritos because he invited her to his favorite Mexican fast food joint and he laughs when she gets mad he tried to eat salsa off her plate.

Two weeks later... Emily still hasn't called back. I guess she wasn't the right girl for me...

No, John. You weren't the right guy for her. You didn't once consider presenting yourself for the occasion, nor did you consider what she wanted to hear. You only did what you wanted to do and it blew up in your face.

This can be applied to writing. Sure, you can expect the reader to "get you," and appreciate your style and voice. Or, you can do your research and gear your writing towards something that will appeal to your readers. This, my friend, is your target audience. I hope with this analogy you realize the nuance between writing for yourself, and writing for your target audience.

No matter how much we might wish it, there is no target audience with "Your Name Here" branded on their forehead (unless you're Matt Damon). You have to understand who will read your books. Are you writing for young adults? Then you need to use phrasing they will understand, situations they can relate to, and characters they will enjoy reading about. I don't care how much you love talking about Andy Griffith, it's just going to fly over their heads and bore them.

In my case, without proper editing I tend to use an edge of purple prose with high, almost scriptural, way of writing. My favorite genre is high fantasy mixed with paranormal, not so much a focus on politics but a turmoil of character emotion. I know it's not what's expected, and I know it's not what people want to read, but that's what I like. Revisions come with a large strain and sacrifice to change my writing from "I wrote this for me" to "I wrote this for you." And just because I have read a few favorite books that accomplish purple prose in their style and were published by the big 5 doesn't mean "Oh look, they did it so I can do it too!" (Namely Earthsea, which is a masterpiece of purple prose in an appraised form.)

Ok sure, there are exceptions, and that's what is so wonderful about this industry. There are no ultimatums. But there is a standard, and unless you're the special 2%, you're going to have to conform yourself to that standard, at least to an extent. And then, once you're established, you'll have the platform and fan base to loosen your belt and relax if you really want to.

I have a good example for this. J.K. Rowling loves to illustrate to her readers not only how subjective the publishing industry can be, but also how it can turn out to be a popularity contest. New writers have to get their foot in the door just like she did, with a lot of hard work, perseverance, and a dash of "right place-right time." Recently on Twitter, Rowling shared her rejection letters from a book she'd written under the pen name "Robert E. Galbraith." She received some comical rejection letters which she shared on Twitter. But what I find interesting is that this novel was not a success...until it was revealed that Robert was a pen name for one of the most famous writers of our time. That goes to show, you first need to build a fanbase, and *then* your success will grow. Writing a good book is only half the battle when it comes to making it in the publishing industry.

So if you find yourself struggling to get an agent's interest, or building up a fanbase, take a good, long look at your work. Did you write it only for yourself? Is this really just an extravagant and well-thought out diary entry? Or is this something you've polished for others to read and enjoy? Have you considered their tastes and expectations?

Ask yourself the hard questions, and then listen to your gut. If you bite your lip and squirm, maybe you need to ask yourself what are your true goals. Do you want to be recognized as an established author? Or do you just want to write what you love, self-publish to put it out there, and leave it at that? There's nothing wrong with either route, but you need to decide which path you truly want to follow.

Is Writing Your Dream? Or Your Goal?

Okay, so if you're still reading I'm going to assume you are telling me you want to write a publishable novel. Congratulations! That's a big step! Writing with the intent to publish is not for the weak-hearted, it's not for the weak-willed, and it's most certainly not for the unambitious. That's why I'm going to inspire you to get through all the tough times by what comes next...

Publishable writing means endless waiting to hear back from agents and editors, rejections by the fistful, and pits of bleakness from which writers wonder if they'll ever emerge.

Wait, I said inspiration, right? That's right, this is the fuel for the moment that WILL come. Every second of desolation is ten seconds of elation for that moment when you hear "yes." That surge of pride when you see your work on the shelves and even that moment when you see a gold sticker that says "Bestseller" next to your name. This image is what awaits you as reality if you are willing to drudge through the trenches to get to the finish line.

So don't be bogged down by the wait times or impossible to decipher form rejections. And certainly don't let yourself be your own enemy by negative talk and demotivation. Remember why you're doing this. Remember your goal, be it reaching others with your message, or simply the recognition of your work as a respectable piece of literature.

If you want something bad enough, and you keep at it, eventually you will reach your goals. It's not about how much you do, it's about how consistent you are and that you don't give up. I don't care if you only write 500 words a day, or if you only edit one page at a time. Maybe you sit in with your critique group once a month. But you're *still* doing it, and if you keep it up then you *will* get there.

There's a difference between goals and dreams. Dreams are a fleeting desire that flutter about in the clouds until they rain down as icy tears. Goals are the path you walk with the prize waiting for you at the finish line, all you have to do is make it there.

3 Tricks to Find Time to Write

Now that you're ready to get cracking, you may be wondering how do you fit writing time in to an already busy life? I'm just like you—a busy person with existing time commitments who squeezes in writing where I can. I have a busy day job, which demands 40 to 60 hours a week. I have a husband and a cat, both of which require love and attention (and I wouldn't change that for the world). I speak with my mother daily, and have friendships I maintain through texting and hanging out. And before injuring my back over the Christmas break, I did yoga twice a week and walked the treadmill three times a week. (Once I'm all healed up I'm going to get back into it—No, really! *Fakes a limp...*)

I consistently write at least 7,000 words a week, and even more on those weekends when my husband was entertained by video games and my cat gorged on tuna and went into a food coma. So believe me when I tell you that even if you're an extremely busy person, you *can* do it.

When I say 7,000 words, I don't just mean a draft of a work in progress. Writing takes many forms. I focus on flash fiction to learn how to condense a story, new chapters to develop a work-in-progress manuscript, blog posts to find my voice and build my platform, and revisions to push toward publishable works. Keep yourself organized and focus on the areas you know need work.

Okay. You ready for the secret to fitting in time to write? Here it is—in three tricks!

Trick 1: Stop trying so hard

There's a fine line between taking your writing seriously and treating your writing like a job. If it's really about making money (which is the core purpose of a job) then you're probably in the wrong profession.

I'll give a real life example here. Someone I knew—seriously, this isn't a story about me in the third person—wanted to write a book. I've seen their work and they were definitely creative and talented enough to write a great book. But what I didn't get is that they saved up all their money and then *quit* their day job to spend a year writing their book. Everyone was pretty shocked, and I admired the dedication. I followed them on social media to see how it went.

They started out strong, sharing passages and things they were learning, but then quickly came to realize how difficult it is to write a publishable book. Their dedication dwindled and they finally gave up commercial writing altogether. I couldn't believe it. How could someone get so far, put in so much investment, and then just give up? But then again, commercial writing is not for everyone. And if you're going to treat it like a job, you're going to lose your passion for it (at least that is the lesson I learned from this instance) or realize you didn't have a passion for it in the first place (which was probably more likely).

I don't want that to ever happen to me. I love writing, and if it becomes a job, then it's time to take a break.

Trick 2: Stop making excuses

Don't make excuses to avoid writing. Don't say "this is too hard" or "I'll never be as good as other authors" or "I just don't have the talent." While there is creativity required, the majority of writing skills can most definitely be taught. To support this comment, I suggest reading Senior Literary Agent

Paula Munier's recent book "Writing With Quiet Hands" to understand what skills can be learned, and exercises you can do to improve them. If you feel like you're making excuses based on a lack of understanding of the craft, this book will help you to be inspired and give you steps to improve your writing. (How do I know? Because I went through it and this book gave me the kick in the pants I needed! Thank you, Paula!)

Here are my suggestions for excuses you may be saying to yourself for those unavoidable time commitments:

Family - They're distracting. I need to spend time with my family and they're more important than my writing.

Solution: Wake up an hour earlier while your family is still sleeping and get in some quiet writing time. Only you know your family's schedule best, and if you can pinpoint a time when you know your family is otherwise occupied, this is an opportunity for you to spend some time on your writing. Even if it's 15 minutes, that's enough to keep your writing consistent.

Work - I can't fit any writing time in during my lunch. That's reserved for *more* work, or eating out with coworkers to build relationships.

Solution: First of all, if you're working through your lunch I hope that isn't a regular thing. If it is, you probably need to reconsider your day job. You're eventually going to burn out or crash and it won't be pretty.

What about work lunches? That's relaxing, right? Yes, but it's also an opportunity to work on your craft! Instead of going out to eat during your work lunch, spend your time reading a book or writing. I know it's considered anti-social, but if these people are your true friends, they'll understand you only want to spend lunch with them once or twice a week, and the rest is reserved for your writing. If they don't understand, then I don't know why you're investing time into those relationships anyway. And if it's for climbing the corporate ladder by making connections, you really don't need to go so heavy on the work lunches. Just make a point to stop by their desk, ask questions about their work and lives, and make valid compliments. It'll go a long way, and help you build work relationships without shelling out cash for expensive lunches.

Going to the gym - I have to choose between working out, or writing.

Solution: I cringe when writers sacrifice their health to find time for their writing. This is a mistake and they'll pay for it later. Don't think that just because you're in motion that you can't work on your craft. How about an audiobook? Part of writing is also reading. While exercising on the treadmill you can listen to an audiobook, or if you're so talented you can read while walking (I've seen people do it but I'll stick to my audiobooks). Or if you're in a quiet environment, you can even make voice recordings to plan out world-lore, character histories, and other necessary pondering that is required for a seamless and believable story. I've also done voice recordings when on a long commute, so even if I'm driving I'm still able to work on my manuscript.

Trick 3: Stop wasting time with social media and TV

I feel silly to have to make this such a big "secret" tip, but I really think it is. I suggest you tally up your time and see how much of it is spent on social media or TV-- which essentially are completely unproductive and brain-sucking activities.

I do find that 5 minutes on social media to solicit followers and interact with existing followers is necessary for a platform, but no more than that is required. As for TV, other than news or an educational program, there's no value being added to your life other than a medium to relax, which you can get by reading too. The only other possible value TV adds is to be able to spark up conversations with other people. But if you're a writer, then your friends are likely writerly people and you'll get a lot further having read books they'd be familiar with.

All that said, don't run yourself into the ground. Find a balance with every point in your life: Family/Religion, Work, Exercise, Relaxation(don't forget to rest your brain!) Make writing another priority you won't sacrifice. Most of all, find satisfaction in your hard work. What do you love about writing? Why do you want to publish your work? Find the real reasons and make those your goals. Be specific. How can you hit the bull's-eye if you don't even know where it is?

That's it folks, the big secrets to finding time to write are out. Only you can decide how to spend your time, and as long as you're spending it wisely and finding a balance between your writing and other time commitments, that's all you can ask from yourself.

Work / Life Balance, Oh Wait... Writing Too!

Now that you've learned how to overcome your excuses, I want to spend some time reinforcing writing doesn't mean you should change your priorities.

Even if you're passionate about writing, it's important to keep a balance. The best way to do that is by having priorities.

1. Top Priority is Family

No matter what you do, as long as you keep family first, you really can't go wrong. Does your son need help with his homework? Don't pawn it off on your sister! Do it yourself. It won't take long and your son will feel loved and appreciated. (Or at least he will in a few years.)

The worst thing we can do is to put other things between us and those that we love. It creates a distance that fills with a moat of doubt, frustration, and anger. Maybe your husband or your wife supports your writing, or your work, but if that's all you do then they will feel neglected. Even if they don't say anything, it doesn't mean all is a-okay. Make sure to spend time for a family dinner or go out for a movie. Pick up on cues if you are frustrating your family by not being "present." As writers, we tend to zone out (that's kind of our job!) but you need to be there 100% for your family. Don't forget what really matters.

2. Health

I debated if health or the day job should be priority 2. I think it depends. Most of the time, health should come first. But sometimes, we all will sacrifice sleep or a meal when it's crunch time. Use your judgment, keep yourself well rested and exercise, even if it's just 30 minutes at the gym. After all, it'll be difficult to write if you're too busy dying from a heart attack.

3. Your Day Job

If you make enough by writing as a sole source of income, or don't need to work, that's wonderful! But most of us have other careers that fund our writing addiction. If you're in the majority, make sure that you're keeping your job your number 3 priority. This also counts if you are a student.

There aren't many things more stressful than not having the income to live comfortably and do basic things you want to do. Some studies go so far as to say the financial stress for those that make less than $50,000 per year can double a woman's risk of heart attack. While any study can be debated for accuracy and longevity, it still surprised me and is worth mentioning.

Having a stable day job will give you the means to have a comfortable life, and the *luxury* of writing. As much as some may want to disagree, writing is truly a luxury. Let me give a prominent example. There was a writer who went to college to focus on the literary arts. However once reaching the higher education, was talked into finding a more "reliable" job and began studying law. Realizing that this was not the path for her life, she dropped out and moved to New York with big dreams. However, writing a book, much less publishing one, can take years. Aspiring authors need to eat. This dreamer took up a job as an airline ticket agent to make ends meet.

It was only when a friend took pity on this author-turned-airline-agent that her writing career got a chance to breathe. Her friend gave her an entire year's worth of wages, saying: "You have one year off from your job to write whatever you please. Merry Christmas."

This gift of a year with the only focus as writing produced "To Kill a Mockingbird," Lee's debut and only novel that has earned her over 45 million dollars (and counting).

While I believe writing can be squeezed in-between the rest of life, I will recognize that if the day-job could be realistically cut, writing a bestseller is on the table (granted that you already have the motivation and talent to do so).

I like to think that if Lee had concentrated on becoming a lawyer, she would have likewise earned enough money and peace of mind to write during downtime and produced her award winning novel. There's a difference between working three jobs to struggle to make ends meet, and having a higher income job in which you will have periods of time to enjoy other aspirations such as writing.

4. Writing

Ok, now we're finally at writing! Did you see all the things that came before? How are we supposed to have any time and energy left? It's difficult, but it can be done. The best way to accommodate writing is to take it in small doses. Give yourself a realistic goal. Write 1,000 words every day. Or make sure to write one chapter a week. If you keep to that rule, you'll have a full-length novel of the average size 80,000 words in less than 3 months! Even if you lowered the bar, only writing 500 words a day, you'll still have an entire novel in half a year. Pretty amazing, huh?

Another thing I like to do is to keep a "muse-book," as I like to call it. When your muse hits you on the head with a great idea, bring out the notebook and jot it down. When you find you have enough time to write, you'll already have a nice little gathering of ideas to work with.

I'd like to say the understanding of these priorities came with inherited wisdom, but sadly, they were all learned the hard way! Isn't that how it usually goes? I hope this guide can help you to realize what's important and help you to balance your writing with the rest of your life. That said, you are an amazing person to be able to do it all." Keep it up, and one day you will meet your goals. After all, there are no experts, only beginners who never gave up.

CHAPTER TWO

Plot Structure

A Formula to a Bestselling Novel

We've gotten our goals set, our priorities straight, our time mapped out, and now we're ready to write. Great! So, what is it that makes a novel successful? Is there a special formula?

I've researched my favorite authors to answer this question.

First on the list: CS Friedman, which is my first favorite because of her dark epic fantasy Feast of Souls.

CS Friedman: Writes from an Outline, not a specific formula, but also follows the DM Rule for world building (To explain what is the *DM Rule*: Basically, if you set a gamer loose in your world, what would keep them from winning or hacking the game?). Her stories are inspired by history and mythology. The plot is solely based on a theme she's trying to exploit. For example, her response to an interview question on a dark fantasy:

Q. *So, since we now know all about Coldfire which other novels/series would you push for new readers and why?*

A. *My current project is the Magister Trilogy, beginning with Feast of Souls and Wings of Wrath. The conclusion, Legacy of Kings, will be published next year. This is a *very* dark epic fantasy in which magic exists, but the cost is so high that it transforms those who use it into something that is...well, I won't ruin the story for you. As with all my works it combines an intense story line and compelling characters with an exploration of what it is that makes us human, and in this case the thematic question, "what price would you be willing to pay for power?". I'm very pleased with the project, and fans* seem to be very excited about it. There are some *major* surprises coming in Book III that I know no one sees coming, that will have everyone running back to reread Books I and II and saying, "Oh my God, so *that's* what was going on!"

-

Source: http://www.bookclubforum.co.uk/community/index.php?/topic/1011 0-author-interview-c-s-friedman/

Also other interesting interview responses that touch on Friedman's writing process:

CC: *You mention that the Elements of Style, by Strunk and White, is an important book for writers to study. While it's clear that a writer should have basic English skills, how important is it to pursue creative writing or other college courses? Is it necessary to have a degree in English?*

CSF(CS Friedman): *I've never taken a creative writing course and I don't have an English degree, so I guess not.*

As a matter of fact, I was turned down in college when I applied to join a creative writing course, because my writing wasn't good enough. The piece I turned in later became a chapter in my first bestselling novel that launched my career. Go figure.

CC: *How carefully do you plot out your stories, is every element conceived in advance, or do you write with a loose outline and let the story tell itself?*

CSF: *Both. I plan things out in advance, but I do it in segments, working from a loose outline and then refining the section directly ahead of me. This allows me to add in stuff I developed as I was writing.*

My story never "tells itself." I control it. In this I differ from many authors, but I think I get the best ending out of a book if I am carefully planning all the hints and clues and plot devices that lead there. Letting the story take control means you don't know where it's going, so you can't do that.
- Source: http://sommerstone.com/sumis/faqs/c-s-friedman-interview-for-cc/

My next target is RA Salvatore, my favorite due to his Dark Elf Drizzt Series:

I won't share his interview here since it's long. To summarize, he is a true "artiste" and "play-er by ear-er." He basically crawled his way up the jagged mountain of publishing and just "writes stories." My kind of dude.

My last target, Mercedes Lackey, my favorite because of her Valdemar Series, namely one about a firestarter in Brightly Burning:

She doesn't even use an Outline half the time. Just writes the story. At least this seems to be the case for her earlier novels. Later, Lackey began to co-author and change up the writing style. While still good books, I did not prefer the co-authored works as I did her original Valdemar Series.

In comes another interview:

Spherical Time: *Can you describe your process when writing a book? How much planning and research does a single work require before you start writing it? Aside from the 40-80 page outline that you've previously mentioned on your website, are there any other patterns that you follow when you write?*

ML: *The amount of research that is required by a book depends on the book. If it is a period piece I can spend months working up to it, getting the feel for the period I need. If it is made up out of whole cloth, as it were, notably high fantasy or contemporary urban fantasy, very little is usually needed. And occasionally I write a book without an outline just to keep my hand in.*
Source   - http://www.writingforums.org/threads/interview-with-mercedes-lackey.2238/

So from my research, my favorite authors don't seem to follow any special formula. But actually, they do. Every bestseller will have a basic formula, just as a delicious cake will have a recipe. Just because your Nana was able to bake it without one, doesn't mean it didn't have a list of ingredients, bake time, and mixing order.

Thanks to a fellow Scribophile member, I can introduce you to the 5 plot points of which will make up every bestselling novel.

1. Inciting Incident

2. "Lock In"

3. First Culmination (basically the SECOND biggest obstacle in your second act)

4. Main Culmination (the Climax)

5. Act III Twist (the thing in Act 3 that turns everything on its head.)
Roughly, the first incident is... first, the lock in marks the end of Act I, the first culmination is the middle of Act 2, the Climax is the end of Act 2, and the Act III twist is...well pretty obvious.

This takes it a step further than my assumption every novel is composed of a conflict, a climax, and then a resolution to the conflict. While the 5 plot points listed above also include this idea, there's an analysis of the plot arc that is going to be present to make the process effective and engaging.

At the end of the day, I find myself agreeing with one bit of advice the most. "There are three rules for writing the novel. Unfortunately, no one knows what they are." - W. Somerset Maugham

The Snowflake Method

Let's say you like the idea of an outline. I don't blame you! In the end it will undoubtedly save hours and hours of fluffy word count you'll never be able to use. Not that I'm siding with plotting versus pantsing, but I'm not going to deny the benefits of outlining.

One of the best outlining methods I've been introduced with is the Snowflake Method. In case you're not aware of the "Snowflake Method," this is an ingenious strategy for how to write a novel in an organized and methodical way-- essentially how to Outline in the least painful way possible. Now, I've written four books, all using the "I'm just going to sit down and write whatever comes to mind" method, aka Pantsing. Let me tell you how that went (spoiler: I've been stuck in the revision stages forever!):

Book 1: Fallen to Grace *(Completed and FINALLY Query-Ready)*

Book 2/3: Excess word count cut from the original *(Heh)*

Time to Write the First Draft: 4 years *(yes I know... But realistically I spent one year's worth of time actually serious about finishing)*

Time to Revise: 2 mass revisions in 2 years *(this can't be normal)*

Words Sent to the Scrap Heap: Over 100,000 *(Definitely not normal...)*

Of course, this was my first book. That's always going to be a learning experience and the first thing you write most likely isn't going to be anything close to publishable. To start with, my first draft ended up being over 170k words. Most debut fiction novels are around 80k words, so I decided to break it up into a trilogy. "Cool!" I thought. "Now I have a whole trilogy!" WRONG! I had a trilogy of crap, that's all.

After joining a writer's group and learning what's-what from published authors, I completely revised the first book. After receiving beta feedback from the revision, I filled in a plot hole for its *second* major revision. Now I finally have something that resembles a readable novel and am currently seeking representation. That journey takes a year all on its own, so I'll get back to you for when it'll actually be available. But for the revision process, I had to basically write an entirely new novel twice with massive changes to prose, plot, added characters, and removed/added scenes. And the two "sequels" I have for drafts will need the same level of revision. I feel like I did this the hard way.

Book 4: Sanctuary *(Undergoing a Mass Revision)*

Time to Write the First Draft: 6 months *(Way better!)*

Time to Revise: I'll let you know...

Words Sent to the Scrap Heap (so far): 15,000 *(Not TOO bad)*

Being my second attempt at writing a book, the draft spewed out like a fountain. That was a blast and I loved it! But now I'm having to undergo a major revision because of beta reader feedback singing a common lamentation. I was even stubborn about it and tried querying a few agents. While this novel was much better received (agents are happy when a book doesn't have angels), they still had some complaints that jived with what my beta readers were saying. So. Okay. I'll stop being a stubborn starving artist about it and do a rewrite.

I have been working on the revision for about 2 months and I feel like most rewrites take twice as long as it did to write the draft. With this logic, I should be done revising next year. While I hope I'm wrong about that, and I am trying to reuse chapters from my original draft, we'll see how dramatic a revision this will turn out to be.

So, bottom line, I feel like there's got to be a better way. I had heard about the Snowflake Method when I started writing Sanctuary, but didn't think much of it at the time. However now I want to be ready for a new strategy when I write my next book, be it a continuation of my current works or a new novel. The Snowflake Method is designed to cut down on future revisions by completely outlining the novel. Just so you're aware, I'm not someone who is exciting about Outlining. Thus, understanding how the Snowflake Method worked piqued my interest. It isn't that you start chugging out an outline like it's homework—you first start with an idea. That's how I work, great! I always just start with an idea.

Once you have the idea articulated in one sentence, you expand it into a paragraph. Then you create character sheets that will fit this paragraph, complete with a synopsis of character arcs, where they start and where they end up, their motivations, everything that is going to drive the plot. The Snowflake Method has SO much focus on the characters, with multiple steps dwelling on this area before moving onto any type of outlining.

What I find interesting about this level of focus on the characters is that it immediately zooms in on a major reason for why I needed to revise my works in the first place. My plot wasn't character-driven, and it MUST be. If it's not, the characters just float around, carried by the current of events and the reader is just going to be bored out of their mind by this structure. As a reader, we don't always realize what's grabbing our interest. We just know that THIS BOOK IS GOOD. As a writer, we must understand what latches a reader in like that, and it's a character-driven plot with narrative thrust (explained in Senior Literary Agent Paula Munier's Recent Book). It sounds so simple, but executing the idea is a lot harder than it sounds.

So I'm going to try the Snowflake Method for my next novel and I am hopeful I won't have to go through so many months of revisions. I'll be sure to let you know how it goes! (In a hundred years when I'm done fixing my pantsed novels of course.)

If the Snowflake Method is completely new to you, Randy Ingermanson made a free explanation on his website, or a complete run-down is available in his book. They both say the same thing, but the book just helps guide you step-by-step with no questions left unanswered.

A Powerful Theme

You've got your first draft! Time to par-tay! And then...time to edit!

When editing your manuscript (and edit you must), it's easy to get wrapped up in spelling, grammar, dialogue scenes and prose. While those are all vital to a publishable novel, there's a big picture you might be missing. I don't just mean the plot arc and character development, but the full message and theme of your novel.

This was difficult for me to grasp at first. I know it sounds simple: what is your book about? But you can't just say, it's about a father and his struggles. Or, it's about a fire-wielding wizard. You need a powerful message that is going to allow your book to stand off on its own. It'll make blurbs easier to write, and if traditionally publishing, it'll be vital to pitching your novel to publishers or agents.

Let's look at the first example:

• A father and his struggles.

This is too vague. What kind of struggles? What is the novel trying to teach or say? Is it about how fathers are underestimated and undervalued? Or is it about fathers who have lost their way? There needs to be a theme that says what is unique about this novel and is going to make me want to read it. Not only that, but makes me feel like I'm going to be able to learn something important from it. It shouldn't just be a good story, it should be a message that the reader can ultimately appreciate.

Second example:

• A fire-wielding wizard.

The fact that the main character can wield fire, and is a wizard, is just a simple vehicle for your message. This actually has nothing to do with your theme. It is simply the packaging you are wrapping around the message. What is the conflict? What are the struggles I can relate to?

If you're like me as I was in the beginning, you write a novel without a theme in mind. The scope is far more narrow. You build up a character from scratch and talk with them every day until they become your best friend. You know them better than you know yourself. You put them in situations that are difficult and challenging, and then, in the end, they (hopefully) get what they were looking for.

But once you reach the end of the novel, take a step back and really try to sum it up for a theme, a message. Maybe you didn't even intend to include one, but you know what? It is an element it needs to have. Especially if you plan on pitching it as a work that an agent or publisher intends to market and sell. A story without a powerful message is going to ultimately be difficult to market.

For example, Twilight. Do you know why it sold so well? Because teenagers around the world could relate to it, however sappy, clichéd or drawn out it was. The message is that a young girl knows she has found true love, and won't let anyone else tell her otherwise, even her vampire boyfriend. Do you know how many teenage girls can relate to that message? People underestimate the power of emotion young girls experience. Perhaps they forget what it was like to be young, or just never experienced it for themselves to fully understand. But it is something like this that makes a story sell. The sparkly vampires were just a pretty package to put it in.

Don't be afraid to realize that perhaps your novel doesn't have a powerful theme to stand on. Take the skeleton of what you have and try to morph it into something that does. Perhaps you only need to add a few chapters to change the message, or maybe you need a full rewrite. It depends on how important it is to you to make a work that people will can relate to, and therefore, a work that will be much easier to market and touch the hearts of readers.

I encourage you to challenge your work. If you find the message it says is confusing, or weak, don't be afraid to make it better. The hard part is already done. You have the story down on paper. You have characters who have come alive and have struggles and personalities of their own. Now you just need to make the manuscript complete with its own message. Don't discourage, you can do it!

PoV - The Impact to the Readers

Whether you have your first draft ready to go, or you're still writing, you may want to consider your novel's Point of View (PoV). There are three main points of view. First Person, which is sitting inside the character's head with pronouns like "I" or "me." Limited Third, which can almost be directly translated from first, but pronouns stay as "he" and "her." Lastly, Omniscient. Omni is how we view most movies where the narrator is the camera. You can't know what characters are thinking and feeling other than judging by what you see.

Before I was a writer, I was a reader. I didn't have the know-how to put into words how PoV affected me, but I realize now how much of an impact it really had on my reading experience.

For example, I read Alan Campbell's: Scar Night cover-to-cover in a matter of a week. I absolutely loved it. But even while I was reading it, I knew it was a little more distanced than what I was used to. At the time, I didn't know why, but now I can say that it's because Campbell writes in "Third Person Limited." Which means the narrator only knows what the main character knows, but it is told as a matter of the narrator's observation rather than seeing the action though the main character's eyes.

Knowing this, it feels natural that Third Person would make it more difficult to connect with the main character. We cannot get in his or her head, we can't feel the emotion and the worries with them. We have to crouch down and observe like a stalker in a dark alley.

When I tried to move onto Campbell's second book in the series, Iron Angel, I was shocked how quickly I lost interest. I rarely put a book down once I begin reading it, but I actually had to stop reading after about 80 pages. So, why didn't I have this problem in Scar Night? In Scar Night, the story is in the "real world", so to speak. The observations are not difficult to comprehend, even in the fantasy world setting. I fell in love with the main character and his awkward personality. Even in Third Person, I was able to emotionally connect. I think this is a triumph for Campbell, that is not an easy thing to do in Third Person writing.

However, in Iron Angel, the world shifts to a more supernatural setting. The "real world" is all but nonexistent. Campbell's descriptions are doing their best to describe the bizarre world around the main character, but without getting in his head and seeing what he sees, I just don't feel as connected. And to add to it, the main character becomes possessed with other souls. How am I supposed to understand how he's feeling and what he's going through? He's constantly conflicted, and I don't always know why. I found I lost my emotional connection with the main character, and therefore my interest.

While this isn't really a review of Campbell's work, which is stellar, it's a great example of how PoV can affect the reader. I've discovered that I'm drawn to books written in First Person. What I don't understand is that this PoV seems to be reserved more for young adult genres. Does it make me less of an adult to enjoy it more than Third Person?

I'd like to think I just appreciate emotional connection more than I do the artistic nuance offered in Third Person. And after writing a novel in First Person, I personally believe that it is much more challenging than Third. It's very easy to overdo the "tell" versus "show" in First Person, as well as avoid an obnoxious use of "I" and "me". Any writer who can pull it off has put in a lot of blood, sweat and tears, and has earned my respect!

CHAPTER THREE

In The Beginning...

5 Mistakes of Aspiring Authors

As an active member of Scribophile, an online critiquing community, I have gotten my share of new-author exposure. I've decided to compile a list here of some of the most common mistakes I see over and over again. I'll avoid mentioning prose structure or grammar/punctuations errors for now, these are mistakes that should naturally resolve with revision and practice. (If you struggle with this, I suggest reading award-winning work and study the writing style.)

Onwards:

1. AVOID: Beginning the story with a sunrise, or the character waking up.

Okay, I understand it may feel natural to begin a story when the day begins. Which would be sunrise, or waking up. But please, NO NO NO NO. The first thing a book should do is hook the reader in, that means something interesting needs to be happening. Waking up is something we all do every day. And nothing is outstanding about waking up to a sunrise, no matter how beautifully described, either.

2. AVOID: Vivid characters with a white background.

This is a big problem I see quite often. Especially for character-driven plots. I suspect the difficulty stems from developing the skill to story-tell in a way that the reader can view the world as you view the world. It's easy to forget that the reader can only paint the image with the tools you provide.

And while vivid characters are wonderful and extremely important, the scene matters too. Not just for fantasy, but any scene needs to be described well enough to make me feel immersed. I want to feel the grass between my toes. I want to smell the ash in the air. I want to hear the cries in the distance.

3. AVOID: Info-dump and main character monologue.

This is a tricky one to avoid, especially for fantasy worlds with wild and complicated settings. It's very difficult to find that Goldilocks Zone of introducing information in an active and interesting way without being overwhelming or otherwise too vague. Even in other genres, I find that there's an info-dump of the character's past, or details of the layout of the house in such textbook detail that I don't see the need. The best advice I can give to this is the same advice given to me, introduce one, maybe two, mysteries at a time. Let the reader zoom in and focus on it. Once we're comfortable with that, introduce something new. It's a novel, not flash fiction. Take your time and introduce compelling scenes; plant in the world-lore and history in bite-sized-bits.

Additionally, if you want to share information, share it actively. Don't tell me she's an assassin, show me she's fingering a blade under her sleeve. Don't say that the youngest son is the least favorite of the family of five, show me the father bringing home presents for everyone except the fifth son.

4. AVOID: A lack of conflict.

This shouldn't need to be mentioned, but after reading quite a few first chapters with absolutely no conflict I'm compelled to point it out. Please don't go on for two chapters describing someone walking through day-to-day life, I'm bored already. And remember, conflict doesn't have to be something dramatic. It doesn't have to be landing aliens or exploding grenades. It can be emotional conflict and internal turmoil. Drag me into the character's head and let me feel what they feel. Let me feel their fear, their anger, their regret. A good story is built on a problem that needs to be resolved. Without that, it's just a report.

5. AVOID: Lack of patience, otherwise known as "I'm awesome"-syndrome.

While not a technical aspect of writing, it's important and key to publishable work. Lack of patience means:

• Poor to no editing: The work is full of grammar errors, misspellings and typos.

• Poor to no revising: The plot has conflicts, meaningless scenes, or boring side characters.

• Low (EFFICIENT) word count: I don't literally mean word count. You can have a 55k word book, but if the filling is not full of efficiently used sentences, then it's not good enough. Each sentence should have proper meaning, details should not be needlessly repeated, and every sentence should add to the entertainment value in one way or another.

If you have any of these pitfalls, don't fret! Edit, revise, tell yourself in the Mirror "I can do this!", wash and repeat.

The Hook: Your Book's Fate Depends on It

All right. Let's get into some nitty-gritty. I don't care how awesome your book is, if it doesn't hook your reader in the first page it won't matter. Have you put as much work on your first sentence as the entire book? Because if you haven't, your work may never be given a chance.

After starting to write flash fiction I've learned the importance of the "hook."

In theory, I already knew a hook was important. There needed to be something interesting to pull in the reader. But what I didn't realize is that the first sentence can decide the entire fate of your book. Snap judgments are made, and your first sentence, first paragraph, first page, will determine if an agent/editor/reader will keep looking for more. This isn't a maybe, this is guaranteed and your entire chance of even being read is determined by such a small portion of your overall work.

This is a classic step in marketing. We're all hooked by shiny objects and exciting one-liners. The cover and the hook is what gets us to pick up the book, and an exploration of the first page is what gets us to buy it.

I started writing flash fiction to get more feedback from professionals. I've been able to get chapter critiques for my novels as prizes from Twitter Pitch contests--which were invaluable!--but I wanted more than that. I wanted to understand my story building flaws. I'm so glad I approached flash fiction to accomplish this goal. I've targeted magazines which give feedback, a list I procured by good 'ol fashion Google searches, literary search engines such as the grinder, and my writer support community on Scribophile. The feedback showed I just took too long to get to the point. If I'm doing that in flash fiction, how is that coming off in my novel writing?

Since then, I've revised my work-in-progress manuscripts for this issue, and they're all the better for it. But I hope you can read this guide and save yourself the months of wandering to reach this epiphany. My advice: Spend an enormous amount of time on your first page!

The First Sentence

There is some freedom of expression on how to format your first sentence. Here are some examples of first sentences of popular novels:

Walking to school over snow-muffled cobbles, Karou had no sinister premonitions about the day.
- "Daughter of Smoke and Bone" by Laini Taylor

Laini goes for the tone approach. We're introduced to the setting, instantly getting grounded in the scene in the first half of the sentence, and then being given an assurance that the main character (with a unique name) doesn't believe anything is going to go wrong, but the way its written we can feel this is sarcastic and everything is going to go wrong very soon.

Everything had gone horribly wrong.
- "TruthWitch" by Susan Dennard

Susan goes for the simple approach. Everything has gone horribly wrong. Simple. Precise. We're ready to go for a ride.

The island of Gont, a single mountain that lifts its peak a mile above the storm-racked Northeast Sea, is a land famous for wizards.
- "A Wizard of EarthSea" by Ursula K. Le Guin

Ursula starts us out strong, giving us the sensation of being in a realm like Lord of the Rings. We're given an overview of a mystical land filled to the brim with wizards, and we're excited to step inside.

When I wake up, the other side of the bed is cold.
- "Hunger Games" by Suzanne Collins

Normally starting a book with the main character waking up is a big no-no. But in Suzanne's case, she's not focusing on the character waking up, she's focusing on what "today" is. Her sister is gone, just like Catniss is afraid of, since today is the "reaping." It's foreshadowing what's to come.

I hate First Friday.
- *"Red Queen" by Victoria Aveyard*

Victoria goes for internal dialogue. In this case, "First Friday" is specific to the world-building element of Red Queen. It immediately jumps into the society's structure and how the main character feels about it. This is the main selling point of this novel, similar to Hunger Games, and Victoria is wise to waste no time and get us going in that direction right away.

Just from the quick analysis of a few first sentences from my favorite books, it's clear that the first sentence has been written with a specific purpose in mind. Usually some vital element is already introduced, or something exciting is said to get us to ask "What went wrong?" or "What's going to happen next?" The best hooks don't just give us information, but set the tone of the novel without breaking a sweat. This can be a pitfall, for if you've set your tone to something which is different than the rest of your novel, your reader will be forever finding their footing, looking for what hooked them in the first place and never finding it.

Here's the first sentence of my novel, Fallen to Grace, which is currently seeking representation.

Azrael gazed down at the child who was so perfect, so serene, she could have been an angel... if she'd still been alive.

I'm going for a mixture of elements taken from Laini Taylor, which introduces the character and tone, as well as Susanne Collins which has a foreshadowing element. I want the reader to be focused on Azrael and her plight. Someone has died, is she next? Are angels real? What does it mean if they are? ... Hopefully it works! Guess I'll find out when the novel is released!

4 Tips for a Stellar First Chapter

Now that you've gotten your first sentence all shaped up, let's work on your first chapter! The first chapter is your first impression, your moment of truth, your novel's chance to sink or swim.

It doesn't matter if you're trying to land an agent, get an editor's attention, or simply sell your book. Whoever picks it up will make snap judgments in the first paragraph they read. If they like it, then they'll get through the first chapter. If they haven't been sucked in by then, it'll be too late.

I recently got a revise and resubmit request from a publisher. The only reason is because they loved my second chapter. But my prologue and my chapter 1 was riddled with issues. The only reason they read that far is because I won a Twitter Pitch contest where it was promised any favorited tweets would be a request for the first three chapters, and they would receive a full review. (I go deeper into Twitter Pitch Contests later in this guide!) I was far more excited about the chance at feedback than actually garnering the publisher's interest, and I learned more than I even hoped. Getting a revise and resubmit request based solely on the third chapter they read only proved to me what I was doing right, and what I was doing wrong.

So now I'm sharing what I've learned with you for what to do and what *not* to do in your first chapter.

1. Do: Be crystal clear without info-dumps

My main problem with this is that I *thought* I was being very clear. But actually, I was trying to shove in far too much world-lore at once. Even if I was able to introduce world-lore through action, it was still too much information. All I managed to do was make it a creative info-dump.
I had a prologue: INFO DUMP. It was a well-written prologue, and interesting, but if you need a prologue at all then just assume it's going to be looked at as an info-dump.

I had the character read a stolen letter as the beginning of the chapter: INFO DUMP

The character reflected over her life while brushing her hair and looking into a mirror: INFO DUMP

What really threw me is that I knew these were borderline info-dump scenes, but I accepted it because I didn't know how else to ease the reader into the world I had created. But that's just not good enough. I don't care how complicated a world is, you will run into the same wall as I did if you make the mistake of trying to explain too much too fast.

2. Don't: be afraid to completely rewrite

I've been through three chapter ones. Sometimes, third try's the charm... If you find that something isn't working, and especially if you can't figure out what it is, try to start the book somewhere completely new. It'll be refreshing to cast off the old piece you've revised twenty times and trotted all over, and have something fresh and new to work with. You can just be yourself again. Don't try too hard, let it come out naturally. Then, when you feel you have something emotionally engaging, polish it up to make sure it's crystal clear for Who, What, When, Where and How. If you have some pieces to choose from, have a critique partner take a look and give you some feedback on which one works best.

3. Do: Include an Inciting Event

There needs to be something to kick off the novel. Even if there's a situation your character is in and needs to get out of, that doesn't mean you can just lead with that. That's the conflict, not an inciting event. There needs to be something immediate and tangible the reader can hold onto. The big picture is not important to them yet. They want a zoomed-in piece of an antagonist or pressing issue they can understand. A car crash...a fight...a history exam... This will propel your story into motion and the reader along with it.

4. Don't: Try to shove too much into your first chapter

This is something I struggled with a lot, and part of my reason for forced info-dumps. Particularly for fantasy. I felt like I needed to give the reader an encyclopedia of this new world and worried they wouldn't understand something. So every time something came up that I knew would cause the reader to ask a question, I made sure to try and answer it.

MISTAKE.

What I should have done is made sure the reader didn't ask the question in the first place. There should be one, *maybe* two major questions that the reader will ask in the first chapter, and they better have an answer. If there are more than that, then you need to start cutting any clue that would cause the reader to ask those extra questions. Save it for later.

If the reader is asking too many questions, they will get confused. If you therefore try to answer all of the questions you've created by the story, then the reader will feel like they're getting an info-dump. It's a vicious tightrope. The best thing you can do is to cut out any superfluous information or objects that would even bring the reader in on world-lore they're not supposed to know yet. That was my key mistake and also why I had so much trouble getting around it. I realized that the reader actually didn't need to know *everything* yet, and it was perfectly acceptable to leave them in the dark until they would be ready to learn more.

I think this is the hardest part about world-building. As the writer, we're passionate about the world we've created and we want to share everything right away. It's kind of like a toddler who finds a new treasure and goes, "Look Mommy Look!" But think about it, does Mom really care? She may find it cute, but that's the extent of it. Do you want to be a cute writer? Or do you want to impress?

I hope this has helped you find the flaws in your first chapter. Sometimes it's not the query letter or the pitch, it's just how the novel is presented. Nothing is more important than the first chapter when making your impression with someone new. Without it, a polished premise and masterful story will be put down. Don't let it hold your story back!

I know that writing can be daunting, and once you've finished your first draft, or even your third or fourth revision, you start to wonder "Is it me?" But don't give up. There are good ways, and then there are better ways, to filter your passion onto paper in a way the reader can understand, connect, and relate. That is the ultimate goal, to help others see your characters and your world as you do. As I love to say, there are no experts, only beginners who never gave up.

CHAPTER FOUR

Character Development

Dos and Don'ts of Character Development

No matter what stage you are in your writing, it's time to look at the character development in your story. I want to point out that character development doesn't start out on the first page, it starts out way before that. There needs to be an entire lifetime, family tree, and culture attributed to your character before they even step out onto the stage.

This doesn't mean that your current work needs to be thrown straight in the bin, no, any character can earn some flair. Sit down and take a moment to consider each of your characters. Sure, it might be a little bit of work. But if it were easy, everyone would do it. (Or so my mother would say.)

Do:

Have a backstory. This doesn't mean that your character needed one before you started writing him or her(although I don't recommend it), but they better have one by the time you're ready to publish. You need to know your characters better than they know themselves. It doesn't matter how you do it, but get to know your characters! And once you do, make sure their story is consistent throughout your manuscript.

Don't:

Have a perfect character. Perfection is boring. Every character needs flaws, especially the good guys. This will make your characters relatable, and more importantly, believable.

Do:

Give your characters unique traits. Get organized. Write out a list of both physical and emotional attributes. Come up with one or two unique quirks that you can pull from and give us an endearing quality to hold onto. Create a pinboard with food they would like or places they would most likely visit. Especially with stories that have multiple characters, it can be hard for the reader to keep them all straight. But the old geezer with the crooked nose, and the long-legged lass, are colorful types that we will easily remember.

Don't:

Forget to give your character a last name. Even I'm guilty of it when I first started writing. What kind of story has a character with only a first name?

Do:

Be specific. How old is your character? When is their birthday? Who are their parents? What's their favorite season? Who are their enemies? What are their goals?

Don't:

Make life easy for your character. Put your character in a situation that s/he's going to hate. Give us a pet peeve or a panic attack. Give yourself an opportunity to help us delve deeply into your character's psyche. The second your character is happy and content, I'm bored and onto the next book.

Bottom line: put in the effort and flesh out your characters to the extreme. If you're just starting out, I suggest making yourself a character cheat-sheet. This will be a useful tool you can go back and reference throughout your novel creation. Or if you're in the revision period, now is the time to expand those characters with vivid background and personality. You will be proud of your work, and your readers will appreciate it too.

Most Common Writing Mistake - Character Development

Whether you're a pantser or a plotter, there is one mistake nearly every writer does, including experienced ones. It's a concept of your writing goal per segment of the book, be it one paragraph, one chapter, or whole sections of the manuscript. When plotting (outlining) your book, you have a series of events carefully planned out. Therefore, it's logical when you're writing that your main goal of the chapter is to meet an event. Which makes the work already sound pretty textbook and dry, doesn't it?

Maybe you need your main character to get into a car accident so he can meet a nurse, his future wife, in the next chapter. Maybe you want your main character to run away from home. Or maybe you're just trying to set up some world lore for your fantasy, and you have a particularly complicated bit of information you intend to teach the reader in this chapter.

Even when pantsing a novel, you'll still have a minor level of outlining going on in your head. You think, okay, what's going to happen next? And then you simply move on to the next plot point. You have these cut and dry goals, and while necessary for the bones of the novel, it's a mistake to write with that as the primary agenda.

While every chapter should have goals to further the plot and delve our readers deeper into our world, there must be one goal above all else: Emotional Impact.

Think about what continuously draws you back to your favorite series. It's probably a list of reasons, but the main one is your emotional investment with the characters, am I right? Without that, it probably wouldn't matter how fascinating or well-written the novel is, if you're not emotionally invested, you're just plain not invested.

That's why when writing, we need to keep this goal in the forefront of our minds. How is the main character taking the events going on on a personal level? What are his or her goals? What motivates him or her to make the decision that leads to the next plot point?

Understanding these character foundations will go a long way with the reader. The reader won't feel like they're just watching the events unfold, but they'll *feel* the events as if it were happening to them. And that's the difference between a flop, and a bestseller.

3 Pillars for Character Development

To get you grounded, let's go over 3 Pillars of Character Development - Achieving Complex and Real Characters.

While any novel will likely struggle with enough Character Complexity, I find that novels with high world-building elements may run into this issue more than others. It's easy to get wrapped up in the world lore, and leave the characters as cardboard cutouts positioned up on a colorful and vibrant stage. While the author likely loves the characters no matter their simplicity, we need *other* people to love them too. (Kind of what my mother always said about me when she was doling out disciplines!)

Pillar 1 - History

Every character has come from somewhere. They didn't just pop into existence when you plopped them on page 1. They had parents, a past, friends, an upbringing, and an entire culture and society who impacted who they are before the novel even starts. Don't forget to thoroughly understand where your character comes from, but also where their society came from. What wars happened, what political regimes rose and fell, what religions dominated and what kind of people from other lands who now reside as minorities, or even majorities, in the place where your character resides.

Most authors have entire notebooks dedicated to this pillar. It's not a matter of what makes it into the book, because when writing you aren't going to include absolutely everything. But you need to have a rock-solid foundation of the world. You need to know it better than anyone else, and at the drop of a hat when your characters are having a conversation and something pops up about a quirky social custom, you need to know enough for why it's there and how your character has been affected by it. It just needs to make sense and seem realistic, otherwise if you're clueless, the reader is going to notice and feel disappointed to be shoved into an uncompleted world.

Pillar 2 - Motivations

What does your character want? And don't make it simple, make it complex. Make the motivations change throughout the novel as your character grows. Start with the initial motivation, make sure you answer why that motivation exists, and how it'll lead to the next plot point.

Example:

Jane is in college to become a teacher. Why? Because she wants to help people. Underlying reason: She really wants to be a doctor but believes she wouldn't succeed.

Next plot point: Her boyfriend finds out she really wants to be a doctor, and pushes her to pursue it. When she finds out his sister has a rare disease, she agrees. New motivations: Become a doctor because that's what she's always wanted to do, but now she can help someone she cares about if she steps up to the plate, believing in herself and what she's capable of.

This is just a brief and simple example, but even here you can see how this development of analyzing Jane's motivations also showed how she grew as a character. That's what is supposed to happen in your novel. That is the essence of "character development" and it shouldn't be something you have to force, but a logical sequence of events that is led by the character motivations. Let me repeat that. The Plot is Led by the Character Motivations.

Pillar 3 - Five Why

This concept is taken from the Japanese standard of asking "Why" five times to really get to the root of a problem. But this really can apply to anything you want to understand deeply. Pick something about your character, either a trait or opinion your character has, and ask yourself

"Why?" five times. This is best explained as an example:

Jane doesn't like apples.

Why? (1)

Because Jane once ate a whole basket of apples when she was a little girl.

Why? (2)

Because her father told her she could only eat one, and she never listens to her father.

Why? (3)

Because she was angry at her father for leaving her mother.

Why? (4)

Her mother cheated on her father, and instead of working it out, her father left when he got
custody of the children.

Why? (5)

Her mother has a drinking problem.

The five why made a seemingly simple opinion go to the heart of the matter. It's an easy exercise to help yourself really understand your characters on a deep and complex level they deserve to have as creations made to emulate real human beings.

No matter your writing goals, be it to provide a message, insight, or just to tell a story, don't miss out on a key component: capturing your reader's heart.

5 Mistakes When Writing Dialogue

You've got a deep, exciting character, but now they need to speak! One of the most important skills a writer needs to have mastered is the proper usage of dialogue. Dialogue provides many things to the reader: Information and Backstory, Character Personality, Plot Flow, Interaction and Dynamic Action.

You may say, well some stories don't have much dialogue. Wrong, what about internal dialogue? Even if characters are not speaking to others, they will most certainly be speaking to themselves.

1. Character's Voice and the Narrator's Voice are Not the Same

This will be most relevant when a story is written in Third Person or Omnipresent Point of View (PoV). The narrator and the character voices will be distinctly different from each other. The easiest way to make sure the narrator does not interfere with the main characters is to give each character enough of a personality and voice that it will not naturally write out as your own. If the narrator and characters start to sound the same, I'm going to get distracted and bored.

Even in First Person PoV, there can be cases where the author may choose to use a narrator instead of the main character, a small hitchhiker inside the main character's head which reports the events. The only instance I can imagine where this would be useful for First Person PoV is if the main character has a thick or jarring accent. I know I'd get a headache trying to read the description of scenery in broken English.

2. Character Dialogue is Consistent

Many writers will use speech style to convey a character's personality. I find this to be a great tool.

If I hear "ain't nobodies by dat name 'ere", I immediately get a vivid picture of the character without any messy narrator description. However there's a catch, the character must always speak this way! Nothing is more jarring than a bumbling accent instantly transforming into polished English.

As we write, it may be easy to forget the character's personality and fall into the trap of writing out dialogue as we would say it. However, you must never forget the character personality you have developed. I encourage you to look through your latest story, if your character has the personality s/he deserves, I guarantee you will find dialogue gaps. Fill those in with the consistent vivid colors your characters are meant to have.

3. Dialogue Tags need to be Efficient

When we read dialogue, our eyes are trained to skim over the dialogue tags (he said, she said, they said). But like anything, dialogue tags have a time and a place. If there are only two speakers, you may want to cut out some of the "he said," "she said." It may be obvious who is speaking, and some of the tags are just in the reader's way.

On the other hand, especially when there are multiple speakers, it's very important that the reader clearly knows who is talking. Don't be afraid to put in a reminding name tag or physical detail to help the reader keep track of who says what. (Critiquing partners are a great tool to find these spots if you're unsure.)

I'll touch on colorful dialogue tags as well (he mumbled, she whispered, they shouted). Some suggest to stay away from these, but I find them strong tools to help the reader understand the tone of the conversation, when used correctly. Read through some of your dialogue, if you find yourself lowering your voice, then it might be a good spot to say "he whispered." Additionally, try not to say "he said it quietly," whispered is much more powerful.

4. Correct and Interactive Punctuation and Formatting

While this is a rather technical aspect of dialogue, it's a very important one. If you have incorrect punctuation, then the reader is going to be frustrated. Keep with established conventions.

As for formatting, keep in mind that how long or short your sentences are will change the feel of the action. If your sentences are short, they will help to convey shock and panic. This will show there's a rush, we don't have time for colorful sentences. Time is short. Danger.

If your sentences are long, they may come off more relaxed and placid, since the narrator has the luxury to ponder such detail.

5. Seize Dialogue Opportunities

This is one that I see many writers missing. Dialogue is your chance to fill in that massive info-dump you've been holding onto! (Or more embarrassingly, made us sit through in Chapter 1.)

It's an amazing cheat. Readers will get bored if information is endlessly drilled through an inner monologue. But if two characters are interacting, suddenly the information is being presented as a forward flow of the story. Something is happening, we are getting to see how these two characters respond to each other, and happily eavesdrop on the conversation like any good stalker would.

I encourage you to go through your latest work and take a magnifying glass to the dialogue sections. The first draft is exactly that, a draft. Keep polishing and your readers will appreciate the hard work.

CHAPTER FIVE

World-Building

5 Pillars of World-Building

I would like to cover some ground rules for fantasy world-building. Fantasy worlds are the reason readers flock to the genre: We live in the real world, why would we want to read about it?

Now, don't confuse this with building a wildly unrealistic world. That's not what I mean. We want a fantastic world... yet is a world that has it own set of rules and regulations. It's okay if gravity is inverted, but you better be able to explain why!

1. How close is your world to the "real world"?

I notice a very popular fantasy trend is "Urban Fantasy." Urban Fantasy is a fantasy world set in modern or "real world" terms. I like to think it is popular because this is how a reader can feel as if the world being painted is actually a possibility. Everything in it seems to make sense: there're coffee stands, people walking their dogs, and oh yes, people flying. It's so close to the real world that that one tiny extra element is intriguing and exciting. Readers can ponder what it would be like if this slight twist were a reality.

Personally, I find this a cop-out. While there are plenty of magical realism stories that even I have loved, (for example, the faerie lore of "Ink Exchange," or teen angel-romance "Fallen"), it's so much more exciting to see an author truly build a world from the bottom-up.

You need to decide for yourself how much work you're going to put into your world. If you want to go the magic-realism route, you have a great opportunity. Make that special fantasy element seamless with the world.

Allow it to be so well integrated that no one will blink an eye. Or, you can go the other route, where the magical element is this wonderfully kept secret that only a privileged few get to learn. But you better make it believable that the secret has been so well kept for all these centuries. After all, we live in the real world and we don't know about it. I like how the TV show "Charmed" did this, they built in a race specifically dedicated to rewind time and undo mistakes when the magical secrets were revealed. Convenient, yet it made the world believable.

If your world is going to be brand spanking new, that's great! I truly applaud you. But be ready to go through a multitude of supplemental notebooks and papers to document your world's vast history and infrastructure. You're going to need it.

2. What is happening right now?

When you start on page one, there will be centuries of world history that's already happened. Don't panic and dump the reader with all of this information. When you were born, did your parents shove a book of world history in your face? No, absolutely not. They gave you what you could handle, and that's exactly how you need to treat the reader. Give them teeny-tiny bits of information. Focus on one mystery at a time. When you immerse us into the world, it's okay if we're a little lost. We are but a newborn babe in a new land. We want to search and explore, and we want to know what's going on right this very moment. We don't care what happened yesterday, or two years ago, or a hundred years before that. We want to know why our father is yelling at us, where did he get that staff? Why is fire coming out of my hands? What's going to happen to me? I need to know the present.

3. What races are present in your world?

Any society is going to be composed of many different races. If you only have one, you're doing it wrong. There need to be different lands with different races that have adapted to those climates. We need to see how these societies have interacted and clashed. What prejudices are there? Why? What are the views of the main character? And it's okay if your main character is prejudiced, we like flaws.

4. Draw a map.

Seriously, draw a map right now. You don't actually have to draw it yourself. There are plenty of online resources dedicated to this aspect of world-building. I can't tell you how much it'll benefit you to have a clear understanding of what lands lie where. Your character will likely go exploring, or be running for his life. We need to have a clear vision of where he's going, what the weather will be like, and what people he can expect to encounter. If you do this before you get deep into your story, it'll help you create that vital sense of realism that must be present.

If you would like some inspiration, look at the first few pages of "The Fellowship of the Ring." You'll be greeted by an array of world maps (like many fantasy novels tend to do). Why do they do this? Well think about it, didn't you enjoy seeing the maps? Didn't it give you a sense of realism that helped you immerse into this foreign world? That's the whole idea.

5. What are the rules?

Again, this world, however fantastical, needs to be grounded. That means there need to be rules. I don't care how wild the world is. I don't care if mages are flying and lizards are singing. You need to explain every fantastic ability. The mages gain their power of flight from the song of the wind. Without the wind, they cannot fly. That's why they live in the mountainous region of (book-lore name). The lizards have human DNA that gave them vocal cords, so thus they can sing day and night just as any human would. But if they mate, they will dilute their DNA and new generations will be unable to sing. See where I'm going with this? With limits, I can believe the world. I can grasp onto uncertainty and suspense for what can go wrong. Nothing is more boring than a superhero with no weakness.

Bottom-line: make your world believable. Once your reader is turned believer, they'll be here to stay.

3 Edits for Backstory and World-Building

Whether you're writing fiction or fantasy, the most difficult pitfall to avoid can be properly fitting in backstory. It's twice as difficult in fantasy because you have to fit in world-lore as well.

I won't go into things to avoid, because it's likely you've already made these mistakes. That's why I'm going to say what you've already done wrong and how to edit it.

1. Info-Dump in Dialogue - As you know, or, remember when?

Let's say you're a little more seasoned in writing, you've read some books, partnered up with some critique buddies, maybe even attended some writing workshops. You've already learned that info-dump shouldn't be present in your story. It's a mid-level writer who will realize they can creatively fit in some backstory or world-lore through dialogue and get away with it (or so they believe). Dialogue is always more interesting than narration, and it's a good move. However there's a pitfall with this, you have to be careful that whatever the characters are discussing makes logical sense.

The easiest way to spot this mistake is by doing a word search for "know" and "remember."

Here's a dialogue example of what shouldn't happen:

"Hey John, as you know, we have a quiz today. Remember yesterday, when we played games instead of studying?" Mike asks.

John nods his head in agreement. "That's right, Mike. And as you know, we'll have to skip class and try to catch the make-up quiz next week."

This is a bit of an exaggerated example, but run a search and you'll probably find a small handful of these no-nos in your manuscript. Characters would never say things both parties already know to one another, and they wouldn't recall an event both characters had participated in. The only time "remember" should be used is if one character is revealing something the other character wouldn't know, and even then, be careful it sounds natural.

2. Info-Dump in Narration - Rambling for the sake of providing information

Narration is fine, but it should be the character speaking to the reader. It can't be a professor reading from a textbook with a monotone speech.

Professor Narration (Don't do it!):

There are two men sitting across from each other in the park. One is thinking heavily, about to make a move on the chess board. The board itself is riddled with minuscule cracks and stained with ingrained dirt. But both men hover over it like it's the greatest treasure in the world.

While in itself, this narration can be interesting, it reads as if anyone could be describing the scene to the reader. Here's the kind of edit I'd recommend:

47

Character Narration (Much better!):

I missed my grandfather, so I went to the one place I could always find him. He loved the park, and because of that, I loved it too. But when I spotted his stone chessboard, I saw two strangers were already playing a game. At first, I wished they weren't there. But as their game progressed, I saw how both revered the small pedestal. While the board itself was riddled with minuscule cracks and stained with ingrained dirt, I admired how they both hovered over it as if it was the greatest treasure in the world. My grandfather would have been glad others enjoyed his donation to the park, just as he always did. I smiled.

Usually "less is more" when considering word count, but in this case if you have textbook info-dump, you'll have to use more words to rewrite it from the character's point of view. If you're looking to beef up your word-count it's a helpful edit, since most edits are about gutting the fat.

3. Transferring Info-Dump from Narration to Dialogue - Info Is Not Relevant to the Scene

Like I mentioned, some of your edits may have been converting info-dump from the narration into active dialogue. Even if the information being provided is information the other character doesn't know, it'll still stick out like a sore thumb if it provides unnecessary details. If the other character doesn't need to know about it, why does the reader?

So let's have a short example of info-dump that was previously in narration:
Ron was married until three years ago. He was married for five years and then divorced after he was caught cheating. His new girlfriend doesn't know about it, and he hopes she'll never figure out his secret. Even though he feels he's changed, he knows his new girlfriend won't believe him.

Converted to Dialogue:
(Ron and his best friend Henry are talking)

"Henry, even though I was married three years ago, I wasn't the same guy then as I am now. I was married for five years. I'm not the cheating kind of guy, but it just got boring."

Henry sighed. "I've only known you for two years, and I'd agree you don't seem like the cheating type. You've been dating your new girlfriend for two weeks, right? That's not very long."

While an exaggerated example, you can probably see that this kind of dialogue just doesn't come off as a natural conversation. Would Henry and John really go into this kind of detail, especially of things both parties already know?

So how to fix it? You need to cut backstory that the reader doesn't really need to hear about. While it's important that you, the author, know all the facts, it's not important for the reader to have a backstory-dictionary for your novel.

Fix:
"Damnit Henry, my new girlfriend was snooping through my phone! Now she's probably going to break up with me."

Henry's eyes bulged. "That's not cool. What'd she find?"

"She found an email I've kept since the divorce. It was from the woman I cheated with."

"Oh man, that doesn't sound good."

The fix doesn't exactly say how long ago he was divorced, how long he was married, how long he's been dating his new girlfriend or how long he's been friends with Ron. But honestly, does the reader need to know all that? No, they don't.

As for the information that Ron has turned over a new leaf, that's part of the "show versus tell" argument. You need to show Ron has evolved in the upcoming plot, don't just tell the reader he's changed.

And with your fix, you've created something for the reader to engage with. Now, the reader is anxious what was in that mysterious email. And will his girlfriend break up with him? Why'd Ron keep the email anyway? This is good, you want your reader to be asking questions, which is defined as "Narrative Thrust" in literary agent Paula Munier's book, "Writing With Quiet Hands." Be sure to keep this in mind that as the plot develops, some of these questions should naturally get answered along the way. The reader wants this world to be a giant mystery they have to piece together. But it shouldn't be a giant mystery that just gets more mysterious.

There's a fine line between making it exciting and divulging little bits at a time, and creating too many questions which therefore frustrates and overwhelms the reader. If you find your critique partners are asking too many questions, don't try to answer everything. That in turn, will just create more info-dump. Instead, go back and edit out anything that would have made them ask questions that aren't really vital to the plot. You need to be in control of the level of backstory the reader learns on their own and how much they actually want to know. Every sentence should be written with the goal of developing the story. Either it needs to make the reader ask an important question, or it needs to answer one. A master writer has controlled every chapter, paragraph, sentence, and word to have a specific purpose and place in the novel. Here are three of my favorites that do a great job at this:

"Dune" : an old classic that does a masterful job of trickling in questions and filling in the blanks for a massive universe full of political struggles, as well as complex characters.

"Lord of the Rings" : would be remiss not to include. Personally, I find some of the narration tedious for Lord of the Rings but for such a complex world it does a great job. Most fans can recite the complicated prophecy and massive cities, races, and political alliances of this world. Some people even learned the made-up Elvish language. Isn't that amazing?

"Fool's Assassin" : a more modern favorite I like to reference from Robin Hobb's Fitz and the Fool Series. What's interesting is I didn't start with the first novel in the multi-series, and it's the novel I'm recommending here. I was not lost in an otherwise complicated magic system and high fantasy setting. I even went back and read the previous trilogy, and still found this one to be my favorite starting point. The previous novels felt more like bonus history. Robin does a great job of introducing elements one-by-one in bite sized bits that are easy to digest. Masterful job.

Bottom line, when trying to include backstory or world-lore, don't get obsessive about it. Keep the mindset on the characters, their desires, struggles, and dilemmas. Pretend each element in your story is a golden goblet or jewel necklace in Aladdin's Cave of Wonders. There are mountains of items to explore, but you led the reader into the Cave completely darkened. Don't overflow the cavern with lava. Light a torch, and guide them through the smallest path, revealing each treasure one at a time until you reach the Genie's Lamp.

F&SF Writers... Do Your Research

It's expected that non-fiction will be the result of extensive real-world research.

But what about fiction?

While not required, conducting research will greatly enhance any novel. You may not expect research for a F&SF(Fantasy & Sci-Fi) novel, but there are many which have done this very thing.

Why? Because while a writer's world will be fantastical and unrealistic, that doesn't mean it shouldn't be logical and grounded.

A great writer will present a world with a reasonable set of limits. Meaning, if a wizard can perform magic, there should likewise be a cost. If a society declares war, there should be a century leading up to such a conflict.

Without logical structure, a world with no limits becomes boring. A war with no deeply rooted prejudice and rich history will have no meaning, and no emotional impact.

Often, a writer will pull from their own experiences to make a great story. F&SF writers create amazing worlds that obviously can never be experienced first-hand. However, that doesn't mean one cannot pull juicy bits from the real world. There is a wealth of human history that can be incorporated into the author's world-building and plot structure. This will paint a picture in which the reader can relate and be a part of. Once a reader is turned believer, great sellers are born.

So wait a minute, if this is so true, what famous novels have done real-world research? Well, I'm so glad you asked! Let's take a look at a few (slightly famous) F&SF stories:

1. Game of Thrones
I wouldn't be surprised if many already knew this, but Game of Thrones has many historical parallels largely based on Medieval European history. In particular, the War of Roses.
Source(one of many, but this felt most relevant): http://mentalfloss.com/article/56558/7-historical-parallels-game-thrones

2. Star Wars
Yes, Star Wars. A wealth of real world religions, cultures and history helped to inspire many of the societies we fell in love with under the moons of Tatooine.
Source: https://en.wikipedia.org/wiki/Star_Wars_sources_and_analogues

3. Harry Potter
While the relation to England based culture is obvious, J.K. Rowling also stated in an interview a parallel is drawn from Nazism.
Source: http://www.the-leaky-cauldron.org/features/essays/issue27/nazi-germany/
or if you rather trust the wiki interview account: https://en.wikipedia.org/wiki/Politics_of_Harry_Potter

So where should you start? It depends on the focus of your novel. To get started, feel free to use the below cheat-sheet.

1. Alien Mind Control or Horror Ghost Possession

What to research? Schizophrenia. Multiple-Personality Disorder. Accounts of real exorcisms (you don't have to believe it, but they're out there.)

Based on these psychological disorders and real world accounts, you can create a character that would realistically show two personalities in one body. You can bring out the symptoms that will have the reader wide-eyed in belief.

2. War Dynamics

What to research? Don't reinvent the wheel, pick up a history book.

This kind of pulls from some of the above novel examples, but it bears repeating. Human history has an unfortunate wealth of information in war. Your war needs to have history, it needs to have landscape and grand scope. What will be the outcome? What brought two societies clashing against one another?

3. Artificial Intelligence

What to research? Today's technology.

This is actively trying to be developed in the real world. What are the current issues and pitfalls? Try to imagine where technology can go to resolve the current issues. Make a world where AI is realistically born and real problems are overcome with logical solutions.

4. Make-believe Religions

What to research? Real world religion and Cults.

There are thousands, if not millions, of religions in the world and wrapped up in history. Each has a rich story and devoted following. What made those people followers? What happened when the group became large? What happened when conflicting religions clashed?

5. Other Plant Colonization

What to research? Real world colonization experience and current issues.

We've already sent men to the moon. What was the first real issue? Aside from the cost and technology, some couldn't even wrap their mind around it and called it a hoax. Would this happen in your world? What current issues do we have to colonize Mars? What will happen when people leave earth and never come back?

There are repercussions to colonization. Take a step back and look at the English colonizing America. What did they do when they encountered the indigenous population? It might as well have been a new planet.

We need to be patient and not rush into a novel. We need to ponder our ideas, pull resources from community and history. Give your novel the attention and polish it deserves!

CHAPTER SIX

Prose, Editing, and Writing Style

Unique Style? Or Just Poor Prose?

The goal of being a writer is pretty simple: Transcribe ideas from Point A (Your brain) to Point B (The Blank Page - eek!). Of course that's stripping it down to its bare bones. (Sorry all bards and minstrels that just rolled over in your graves.)

So now the magical question, how do you accomplish this goal? There's not one thing that makes a writer successful. Yet, it's safe to say prose is the vehicle in which our writing is delivered and plays a large part in success or failure. For some, it may even be the deciding factor between acceptance and rejection.

Let's assume your premise is breathtaking and powerful, the Queen of England as a passenger in your vehicle of prose, so to speak. But, if she's delivered in a 1990 Chevy Lumina (one of the most hideous cars of all time), there won't be adoring fans falling over themselves to greet you. You need your prose to be a spectacular Tesla Model S, a dazzling Lamborghini Aventador, a killer Porsche Spyder!

Prose is a skill in which we convey our story through language in a creative and enticing way. So, if you've been rejected by agents or publishers based on your prose, that's actually a good sign. It says nothing about you as a writer other than you have not developed the craft as much as others. It says nothing of your creativity, zest or talent for writing as a passion. Prose is a skill that can be learned. All you need to do is study. Isn't that great news?

There's one catch, you first have to accept you're less than awesome.

This section's focus: Know the difference between Unique Style and Poor Prose.

This is the top amateur writer mistake when it comes to prose. Let's use a fictional character as an example.

Jane has been writing all her life as a hobby, but finally wants to take it seriously. She's written a novel and the second she types out "THE END" in her word document, she gives her cat a high-five, prints it out at Office Max and she sends it off to a publisher. Three months later it comes back with one sentence of feedback: "Improve your Prose."

She's baffled, partly because she doesn't even know what prose means. So she looks it up on Google.

"Prose: written or spoken language in its ordinary form, without metrical structure."

She thinks to herself, "What the heck does that mean? Gosh, I don't know anything... I know! I'll join a writer's critique group. They'll be able to help me."

Jane heads to her first meeting at her local bookstore. She shows the rejection letter and they knowingly nod and say, "Ah, the first heartbreak hurts the worst, eh? But let's have a look here. Prose. Hmm. By definition, prose means the act of writing anything that's not poetry. But if a publisher tells you to improve your prose, then you just need to advance your writing skill."

It sounds like a vague answer, doesn't it? That's because prose is one single word that encompasses all of the millions of possible ways sentences/descriptions/scenes/paragraphs/chapters/.../etc! could be structured and described. It is one of the most underestimated skills a writer has in their toolbox. If you have mastered prose, then you have mastered the skill it takes to convey your story.

But sadly... Jane doesn't understand that. She shrugs off the mumbo-jumbo and invents her own reasoning. *Maybe the editor didn't read far enough... Surely he would have liked Chapter 6 where there's an interesting twist? Maybe he's a sexist and didn't like a female heroine? Yes! That must be it.*

So, Jane offers her first chapter. She's sure that this time, everyone will get how great her story is.

The writing group eases her into a short list of amateur prose mistakes they can already spot. "Well, Jane. Since the editor thought you needed to work on your prose, let's start with this... You see how you wrote three sentences in a row that all started with 'I'? Try to rephrase it without doing that. When telling the story in first person, it's an easy mistake to make. Everybody does it on their first try."

Jane frowns, and doesn't feel that should matter. It's about the story, not if she started a sentence with "I". *I mean, it's first person! Of course sentences will start with "I"!*

But she nods, hoping they think she's taking their advice. She wants to know why her story isn't exciting for them. *It's got to be the plot, right?*

Then, another member points something out. "You keep repeating the same words. Maybe try to vary it up a bit?"

What... Because I wrote "She picked up the raincoat before running out into the rain"? How else am I supposed to write it? It's a rain coat... for the rain.

"What about this? You have quite a few run on sentences. You use commas instead of periods. And you're using such flamboyant words. Why not keep it simple?"

Jane jolts to her feet as she presses the pages to her chest. "That's my *style*. It's how I write. And if you don't like it, then that's your opinion. One which I don't agree with." Jane thinks that no one is "getting her" and rushes out, never to speak to such close-minded writers again.

And that's why... you've never heard of Jane.

Bottom line, when someone defensively says their way of writing is their *style*, then that usually means they're making an excuse for poor prose. It also means they don't intend to change, which is as good as saying they have no plans to be taken seriously as a writer. "You just don't get me." or "It's unique." Yeah sure, the hand painting I did when I was two was pretty unique, but you're not going to see that reprinted and sold to thousands as a world famous piece of art.

I know it's a hard pill to swallow. We've all been there. And it can be confusing when friends or family tell us how impressive our writing is to them. But they're not editors...they're people who love you. While it's fine to try family and friends for a quick beta read, by no means should they be considered the sole expert on good writing unless they are professionally in the field. Join a writer's critique group, go to a writing workshop, or pitch your work to publisher contests where the reward is feedback or critiques. You'll find out where you truly stand.

Prose is just like any other skill. There are techniques to follow and common pitfalls to avoid. I hope you'll join me as we study the world of prose together. But first, in order to address these issues, we must understand prose and approach it with an open mind. That's why I've dedicated an entire section to this very thing. We can't fix what we won't admit is broken, nor what we don't truly understand.

5 Common Pitfalls in Prose

The first time you took pen to paper and tried to write a story it's likely that it came out simply as information. It takes time to rewire the brain to spit out information as good prose. The best way to start is by understanding the major pitfalls of dull writing.

For this section's tips, I'll use this example.

Poor Prose (51 words):

Mike quickly walked into the half-burnt living room after the fire. Looking to his left, Mike was sad as he walked to the piano stand. It stood in front of him and he considered its burnt surface from the fire. Putting his hand on it, he felt the cracked leather.

Good Prose (29 words):

Bursting through the front door, Mike stumbled to the piano stand. He collapsed to his knees and ran his fingers across the cracked leather. The fire had destroyed everything.

Before I get into the pitfalls, I want to point out one major thing. Notice the word count? The second scene is almost half the word count, but don't you feel like it said so much more? Whenever you edit, your word count should be lower but your content should actually be more.

Pitfall 1 - Filtering

Filtering is when you describe what the character experiences as if you aren't the character. In the example, Mike considered the piano stand. But that's actually redundant information. As long as the Point of View (PoV) is first person or close/limited third, then anything that is being immediately described is therefore experienced through the character. I can simply have Mike interact with the piano stand or describe it (cracked leather). I don't need to say he felt it, because if he's touching it, then I already know he can feel it.

This may be a difficult concept, so let's try another. I said that the piano stand stood in front of him. But actually, there's no need to point that out. If the piano stand is described at all, we know that it's in Mike's vicinity. And especially if he is interacting with it, then we know it's in front of him for sure. There's absolutely no reason to say "it stood in front of him."

Pitfall 2 - Specifying where a character is looking

I see this one all the time as I critique drafts of beginner writers. In the example, Mike looks to his left. Why do we need to know that? It may sound simple, but I guarantee your work has this issue somewhere in some shape or form. "She glanced to her teacher" "She looked around" etc. As long as the PoV is either in first person, or limited/close third person, anything being described is already what the main character is experiencing.

In this case, if Mike is interacting with the piano stand, or if the piano stand is described whatsoever, then we already know Mike is looking at it. And even more so, the reader really isn't going to care if the stand is on his left or right unless he's throwing a right hook at it.

Pitfall 3 - The scene isn't immersive (not using available senses - sight/smell/sound/touch)

If your readers aren't getting into the story, it's likely because you haven't made it *feel* like they're really there. You need to paint a story not only with plot and images, but also sounds, smells and tactile sensations.

In the example of poor prose, we're just told that the piano stand is old. But isn't it better if the reader can come to that conclusion based on what they're feeling through the character? Have your character touch things, smell things, explore the world with all of your senses.

You don't have to get too carried away. It would have been a good opportunity to add in how the smell of burnt material affected Mike in the example. But we don't want to get bogged down in the details, just paint a picture and move on. (In a longer version of the scene, smell could definitely come into play.)

This can be paired with the old "show versus tell" argument. In this case, the author just told you the piano stand was old instead of proving it to you. If you often tell the reader aspects of the story instead of letting them come to the conclusion on their own, your story will be hollow and unbelievable. The reader just won't be convinced.

Pitfall 4 - Using inefficient/repeated words

Every word counts. Don't be redundant and don't use a vague term when you could use a descriptive one. Inefficient words include adverbs when a strong verb will work better, repeated words, and vague terms.

Adverbs:
Adverbs actually have a time and a place. The general rule of thumb is 1 adverb for every 250 words. That's the average in traditionally published novels. This doesn't mean you need to go through your work and strike out all adverbs, though it would be a start. Basically it means that adverbs should only be used when a strong verb just won't capture the intended meaning. It won't happen often, but there are a few limitations where an adverb will describe the scene best. Until you're able to master it, try to keep to the rule of thumb 1/250 until you're advanced enough to break it.

Repeated Words:
In the example, the words "fire" and "walked" are used twice. It makes the reading tedious and boring. Even if you feel it's difficult to find a different word to use, get creative! Don't bore the reader with something they already know. The work not only needs to be informative, but also entertaining.

Vague terms:
We want to know that Mike made his way over to the piano stand. He can simply walk there, or he can stumble, jaunt, skip, or bolt his way there. Depending how his motion is described with this vital verb, we'll get a different impression of how Mike is feeling. He stumbled, he's frantic and upset. He collapsed to his knees, he's heartbroken. We believe him and we empathize because he's showing us how he's feeling instead of expecting us to believe the narrator.

3 Levels of Prose Edits

Unless you're a professional writer who's been writing every day for years (and knows what is considered publishable writing), then I wouldn't suggest worrying about prose the first draft you spit out. The critical aspects of your writing are your voice, your creativity, and writing from your heart. The first draft should be full of errors and "bad writing," because it's about the content, not the presentation.

I think one of the first mistakes writers do when they first start out is get done with their first draft and think "the hard part is over!" It can be quite the wakeup call when a writer learns that the draft most likely is the easiest, fastest, and most painless part of the process. I know people who can spit out 5k words a day or even more without breaking a sweat. But however long it took to write it, it should take maybe twice, or even three times as long to edit.

The reason is because once you start getting into the editing process, you're analyzing not just prose but sniffing out plot holes, scenes that don't push the story along and erroneous information that just needs to be cut. I just want to focus on the prose portion of editing, since really I think it's the part that can take the longest.

Let's divvy up how to approach prose-editing in three levels. Beginner - Middle - Advanced

1. Beginner - Worry about Prose Last With Outside Help

When just starting out, prose is not something that's going to come naturally. There're going to be a ton of adverbs, places where you tell instead of show, and laundry lists of adjectives for apparently no reason. Just accept the first draft as the good, bad, and ugly that it is.

But whatever you do, don't expect to do the rewrite on your own. You need someone else who knows more than you to look at your work and tell you what's wrong with it. I don't mean your sister (unless she's a professional editor), and I don't mean your friends because they'll just want to tell you how great you are. And you should be disappointed if that's the kind of feedback you get, because it's not going to help your work get better.

If you have the funds, the fastest way to shape up poor prose is by hiring a professional editor. Do your research and find an Editor with an impressive portfolio of published authors. There are a ton of self-proclaimed freelance editors out there, don't be suckered into one of these schemes just because it's cheap. At best, you're going to get someone who mildly knows the craft and will have mild feedback to give you in return for your hard-earned money. At worst, you're going to get someone who'll disappear after the funds have been transferred.

A good resource is *Reedsy*, kind of the LinkedIn of the self-publishing and Freelance Editor world.

If you don't have funds to spend on your writing endeavors, have no fear, that's not a problem. Whether you hire an editor or go the secondary route of critique partners, the only difference is the amount of time and effort YOU need to put in. And earning that money in the first place took time and effort, so if you look at it that way, both routes require the same amount of commitment.

The second route is joining critique groups. Usually you get a mixed bag of amateurs and professionals from this type of setting, but with enough effort you will find people who know more than you do and can help you with your craft. The catch is that you're expected to return critiques. In some way, this is an invaluable experience. You can learn how to improve poor prose just by editing someone else's work. You're not emotionally attached and when you experience someone who just won't listen to logic, it'll help you realize if perhaps you're guilty of that yourself.

If you're unsure what kind of critique group to join, just try out a few and see what works for you. Be this an in-person critique group or an online one. I personally use Scribophile.com, an excellent resource for amateur and professional writers. There are others out there but I've yet to find one that works better. I also use an in-person workshop with professional authors that attend, but the downside for that is they only meet twice a month, so it's excruciatingly slow.

Notice for the beginner level, I don't even suggest self-editing. It's just not a good idea. You need someone to point out what mistakes you're doing, since it's most likely you have a handful of favorite errors that you'll just keep doing over and over again until you retrain your brain to structure the sentences differently.

2. Middle - Iron out Prose during the Revision, supplemented by Outside Help

Once you've been around the block for a while, and you'll know when you're at the next level, it's time to start your self-edits when it comes to prose. I still recommend focusing on prose only on a revision level since if you try to do it during the draft you'll start to worry more about prose and less about content, and that's not what you want to do.

I still recommend getting an extra set of eyes on the work since everyone is impossibly dense when it comes to finding even the most simple flaws in their own work. You may think you've ironed out your prose to a high sheen, but all it takes is one other person to look at it to realize how wrong you were. (Speaking from personal experience here!)

3. Advanced - Keep Good Prose as you Write the Draft, Use Beta Readers for Final Check

Now, once you've been writing for a really long time, you can start to know the rules of prose so well that even when you're writing the draft you start to nip mistakes in the bud. You even know what you want to focus on, so you incorporate beautiful prose along with your developing premise. Even so, a first draft is a first draft and should be treated as such. The first time words hit the paper is not a finished piece, so be sure to get either beta readers, critique partners or an editor to give it a nice comb through for typos and other mistakes.

Even if you're not really at the "advanced" level, I do have a trick I recommend for making the revisions easier. When I'm writing a draft, I start first by hand. And as I go, I will already recognize what words or sentences just aren't going to work. But instead of trying to fix them right there, I just underline it and continue on with my draft. Then, when it's time to type it out on the computer, I can do a nice first revision with the rough points already marked. I just follow the guide I've made for myself and rephrase or rewrite anything that has an underline. So far, it's made my first revisions pretty successful and it's a technique I'm quite happy with. I recommend trying it even if you don't like writing by hand.

Get Some Distance

No matter how much you've poured over your manuscript and polished it until it shined, there is one more thing you can do to make a difference. You can walk away. (But make sure you come back!)

This concept may seem simple, but is paramount to improving your prose if you find yourself really getting stuck. This is a technique when you've edited until you can edit no more, and no matter what you do, you can't seem to polish your manuscript that last 10%. There's something wrong, something not smooth. And for the life of you, you can't figure it out.

Maybe you're saying, but AJ, my first draft is pretty good. I don't need to edit it until it's clinical. Well, let me tell you this. When you write out your first draft, that is going to be the purest, true to yourself, THIS IS ME moment of writing.

But guess what? The natural you is full of flaws, typos, and redundancies. I'd make a nudist/hippy reference, but I don't want to offend anyone. (Too late.)

So, your draft needs a good scrub. Nothing wrong with that. You sludge into the muck of your manuscript and scrub-scrub-scrub. After a while, you think it smells pretty nice. But after a beta reader or two, you'll get back some complaints that the prose wasn't up to snuff. But how's that possible? You can't smell anything amiss.

Think about the last time you walked into a stinky room. At first, it was like "Phew what is that!" And then, it started to smell normal after a little while, right? That's how an over-edited draft becomes. You're so close to it, so "surrounded by the stink" that you can't even smell it anymore. There's only one way to fix that, and that's to get out of the room until you regain your sense of smell.

Once you've walked around in some clear air for a while, maybe smelled some other things, roses, daffodils, what have you, come back to your slightly-stinky manuscript. You'll sniff in every nook and cranny and you'll be surprised what you couldn't smell before now seems perfectly clear. There's a rotten apple under this rug, or there's a dead raccoon in the corner "HOW DID I MISS THAT?"

I know this metaphor is a bit gross, but it works! Put your manuscript down, I'd recommend at least two months. Six would be ideal. (Yes, I said six.) You really need to get away from it long enough to change your mindset. Unless you have a photographic memory, this technique will work. You'll transform into the one thing you crave feedback from: a reader. Once you have some distance from your novel, the more you'll actually forget what you wrote. And then, when you come back to it, you'll read it as a reader would. You'll catch places where a reader would trip up, or sentences that just don't seem to flow or make sense.

I know it's hard to imagine working for a year+ on your sweet baby-novel and then putting it down, but this is an opportunity to work on something else. By no means should you stop writing. Depending on your goals, there are plenty of other activities you can do in order to progress as a writer. If you want to make your bio section of a query a bit more fluffy, join a fancy writing workshop, work on some flash fiction or poetry and submit to some reputable magazines, or even a short story competition. If you're really rambunctious, work on a separate novel. Whatever you do, do not even think of or pick up your manuscript for, at minimum, two months. Six months would be best. (Yes I'm repeating that because it's important.)

All that matters is that you put it down for a while, and come back to it when you're ready. This doesn't mean use it as an excuse to shove it under the bed and forget it ever existed. That would be called giving up, and you're no quitter. No, this is about patience and determination. One of the many tools you will utilize to become the writer you are striving to be.

3 Prose Edits You Should Know

Last year I ran a blog series called the "Journey of Prose." This was successful mostly because I don't think a lot of bloggers focus on the writing craft itself. Why is that? Because it's difficult and controversial. There's no real right or wrong answer when it comes to good and bad prose, but there are some general guidelines which will determine where you stand.

When someone is reading your work, maybe just a beta reader or a friend, they might not be able to express what they don't like about your story. That's because they aren't aware of the technical differences between books they love to read and yours. That difference 99% of the time is going to be prose

Novel Writing is its Own Language

Novel Writing is the written expression of language to tell a story. That means it's not sitting around a campfire telling a tale, and if you write that way it may or may not be successful because rules can be broken, but generally it's a specific method of communication unlike anything else in our society. And if you've not read many books, how on earth are you supposed to know this secret language of novel writing? The only way to learn a language is to immerse yourself in it, so start reading and start reading now. The language of novel writing has its own rules, just like any other language. There are going to be certain ways to form sentences to get your meaning across and it can't be like a textbook, without color or art form. And it certainly can't be something you'd blather on to a friend, because real life dialogue is filled with irrelevant statements, repetitive sentences, and awkward pauses. Writing a book needs to be one thing above all else, efficient.

Word Choice Efficiency

By efficient, I mean each word in the story has a specific purpose. A reader is spending their precious time to be entertained and easily envision the world. Filler words or weak nouns are going to make them feel cheated and confused.

Think about one of your favorite books. If you've zipped through that book in a day, and went "Wow! That was the best book ever!" I hope you now realize for the 3 hours you spent reading (if you're a fast reader), the author probably spent 3 *years* not just writing, but perfecting, that book. It was easy to read because it was *designed* to be that way.

Prose is the last edit that's going to happen when an author is writing their book. There are a bunch of developmental edits that should take place before prose becomes a concern. After all, what's the point in icing a cake before it's baked?

I'm sure there are authors out there who write out their first draft, and immediately try to shop their story. They may imagine: "Agents will recognize if this is a story they'll like. An editor can help me revise for the nit-picky stuff." If that's you, time to turn over a new leaf. From the words of Senior Literary Agent Paula Munier in her recent book "Writing With Quiet Hands" literary agents want a book you can bounce a dime off of and is ready to rock the reader's world. They don't want a fixer-upper. Writing craft is probably the first thing they're going to look for, and if it's not there, you're going to get a form rejection and never know if they would have actually been interested in your story.

When it's time for a prose edit, depending on the quality of your draft, it should take at least half the time it took to write the draft, if not more. (This is purely for the prose edit. Developmental edits should generally take three times as long as it took to write the draft.)

I recommend doing these three prose edits to get you started. Try to spend some serious time on this. The more it's polished, the easier the manuscript will be to sell. Imagine it's a diamond, and you're cutting and polishing so that it sparkles like one of those Zale's rings you see on TV.

Three Prose Edits

To get you started in your prose edit, I'm recommending three run-through revisions you should do. These are just a bare minimum, and I'd recommend schooling yourself on prose before attempting a prose edit.

Prose Edit 1: Filler Words

This is probably one of the fastest and most helpful sweeping edits you can do for your prose. Open up the search box and start finding your overused and filler words. You'll either be able to simply delete, which if you can do that without changing the meaning of the sentence it's certainly an unnecessary and inefficient word, or you'll need to strengthen a weak noun or modifier. Quick example: "little bird" should be "finch."

- Suddenly (It's a lot more sudden if you just say what is happening)
- Then
- Just
- Very (This usually is pointing out a weak modifier)
- Really
- But
- Almost (Do or do not, there is no try)
- Slightly (Be confident in your descriptions)
- That (This is a biggie. Bet your word count falls by 500 words just taking this out)
- As you know (If everyone knows it, why is this being said?)
- Not (This means you should have used a contraction. Unless your characters are British, or Yoda, they   should be using contractions.)
- Little (weak)
- Big (weak)
- Large (weak)
- Up (He stood up. Guess what, you can also simply say "he stood")
- Down (He sat down, or, he sat!)
- Any filter words such as See/Heard/Felt/Realized/Watch/Look. Simply describe the scene. We don't need to know your character is seeing/hearing/feeling because being in their point of view already tells us that.

Once you get the hang of it, you'll start to spot unnecessary and filler words on your own. Make sure every word in your sentence is there to convey meaning, and isn't simply taking up space and killing your readers' enjoyment. A simple rule is if a word is taken out and the meaning of the sentence didn't change, it shouldn't be there.

Prose Edit 2: Boring/Irrelevant Information

This one is a bit harder to spot. When storytelling, the only information the reader wants to know is why should I care about this character, and what is going on now that is developing the story? Anything else is boring information that they will probably want to glaze over. Here is a list of boring information you'll want to try and avoid.

• Excessive Narrator Monologue
   ◦ Those times when the narrator is staring out a window just thinking about life. This can go on for pages just talking about their family, their dreams, or just what they had for breakfast. Keep such musing short, or altogether absent. Most of the time you as the author may need to know this information to make a cohesive story, but the reader doesn't need to be privy to every detail.

• Play-by-Play
   ◦ A novice writing mistake is to describe every single movement going on. The character walks to the door, looks at it, turns the knob, steps across the threshold, takes a breath, their heart beats twice... Did we really need to know any of that?

• Flashbacks/Remembering Past Events
   ◦ I hate flashbacks with a passion. If something is so important that the narrator needs to take us back in time, maybe the novel should have started earlier and described these events to us live. Time jumps are confusing, disorienting, and lazy. In the case of the main character remembering something, the narration will usually be in the past or past perfect tense, requiring a lot of "had" and "was" which can also become annoying to read.

• Laundry List Descriptions
   ◦ Unless you're writing "Daughter of Smoke and Bone" and you're trying to help the reader picture a Chimera, don't go on for a whole paragraph describing what a character looks like. Focus on one powerful image, such as *"she leaves the house without mascara."*(Source: P. Munier.)

Do you see what these key points have in common? They are all things which don't move the plot forward, but rather give the reader unnecessary information. Prose is not just about what you say, but how you say it. (I've been waiting forever to use that line!)

Prose Edit 3: Repetitive Words and Information

There are two major forms of being repetitive in writing. One is simply using the same word twice or more within the same paragraph or page. If you say the "wind rushed," you shouldn't follow the next sentence with "she rushed." It'll become bothersome and annoying for the reader and make your writing seem lazy.

The second type of repetitiveness is giving the same information twice. Maybe a description repeats itself, or more commonly a plot point is brought up multiple times. Sometimes this is on purpose, but try to give your audience some credit. They're smart people, and you don't need to keep pounding the same information over and over again. Say it once, and move on.

Filtering - You'll Distance Your Readers

I've mentioned filtering earlier in this guide, but now I'm going to go deep and make sure you understand what it is, and why it's vital to erase from your novel.

When I first learned of it, no one introduced the term. I received an unholy amount of critiques/beta reads come back on my work complaining how the reader felt "distanced" from the main character.

"I want to know what she's thinking! I want to get inside her head!"

Now, this confused me to great lengths. The work is First Person PoV and I even denote thoughts through italics. You are literally inside her head!

After receiving the same complaint over and over, I gnashed my teeth, and then dove into the critiques side-by-side. What did all of these have in common? I know the critiques are picking up on something I'm doing wrong. Something in the sequence of words is describing the events from far away, rather than from the main character herself.

Then it hit me. I was filtering. Below is an example of before and after revision.

Before
I felt annoyed that he would continually go over the same spot, but I didn't speak a word of complaint. I felt sweat trickle down my brow as the smoldering fires slowly crept up the length of my back. The minutes dragged on endlessly as he continued his work. Minutes turned into hours, endless hours. I felt my heart racing as I panted through the pain.

After
I gritted my teeth in annoyance that he would continually go over the same tender spot, but I didn't speak a word of complaint. Sweat trickled down my brow as the smoldering fires slowly crept up the length of my back.

The minutes dragged on endlessly as he continued his work. Minutes turned into hours, endless hours. My heart raced as I panted through the pain.

I think you can see the pattern. Instead of saying she was annoyed through action, I told the reader that she felt annoyed. By doing that, we are stepping back and being told a factual state about the character. But, when we hear an action: she gritted her teeth, we can feel her annoyance. And in other cases, the "felt" could be removed entirely. It only served to distance the reader as secondhand information, instead of immersing them into the action.

Filtering is not just limited to the description "felt," but also "saw," "heard," and even time lapses such as "suddenly" or "quickly." Do you really need to mention that your character heard a voice in the distance? Or can you simply say that there was a voice carried by the wind?

Do you need to say: "Suddenly, the doorbell rang?" I don't think so. It'll be much more surprising and sudden if the doorbell rings without being verbally warned.

This concept is a bit more advanced. Comb through your manuscript and see where you can remove such notations that let us know the character saw or heard something, and just state it as a fact. If we are already in First, or Third Person Limited PoV, we are seeing the world through the character's eyes. This means that any action being described is automatically seen or heard by the main character. In most cases it's going to be redundant to point it out.

Quick and Dirty Editing

Even after getting distance and revising your novel as best as you can, you can't beat a third party opinion. But don't just throw your first draft at your little helpers, make sure to save everyone's time by cleaning off the grime so they can find the cracks in the foundation.

So often when we approach the first draft of our novel, it's with a sense of dread and foreboding. A novel is a massive thing to tackle and all kinks can't be ironed out on the first try. That's why we hand off our newborn to editors, beta readers, and critique partners.

It's a mistake to just hand over your first draft. There should be some editing involved before you expect someone else to invest their time in poking holes in your novel. I don't mean that you should spend months shaping it up as much as possible with your own set of eyes and your one-sided perspective. But rather, there are glaring flaws that can be fixed that should already be out of the way before it gets to your reviewer.

An editor/critiquer and especially a beta reader will only be able to pinpoint the first or second layer of grime on your novel. You'd be doing yourself a favor by cleaning that layer off so that you can get to the root of the issues instead of minor things you could have fixed on your own.

I like to believe this is why we never get it right after the first revision. Once we fix one problem, three more will appear. It's not because they weren't there before, but rather in comparison to the other issues they fell in the background and we didn't have the capability to notice them.

Just because you fixed all the issues that were caught the first time around doesn't mean the novel is perfect, so by all means be fully prepared to go through multiple revisions, even rewrites, of your novel before you finally get it right.

Now for some quick and dirty tips before your novel changes hands.

1. Filtering

This was introduced earlier in this guide but I'll reiterate and give some other reasons why it's something you don't want to be doing. This is a simple prose mistake that can be detrimental to a novel. While it's a no-no for any PoV, it will have the most destruction in a first PoV novel.

What is filtering? Basically any sentence that says the character "saw, heard, felt, knew" something. Ninety-nine percent of the time, the PoV already tells the reader whatever is being described is automatically saw/heard/felt/known by the main character. Therefore, if you outright say "He saw his sister get into the car." then it turns out to sound pretty repetitive. You could simply say, "His sister got into the car." It also shortens up the sentence, which brings us to our next point.

2. Keep it "Crisp"

If you notice comments on award winning novelists, a favorite compliment is "crisp" writing. What makes writing sound "crisp"? I like to think that the author managed to find the shortest way to say each sentence that still kept it fresh and appealing. The reader doesn't like to feel as if their time is being wasted. They want a story, and they want it in an entertaining and efficient way. Superfluous information, and more so, superfluous descriptions, are a waste of their precious time. Superfluous information, and more so, superfluous descriptions, are a waste of their precious time. We've already mentioned word efficiency and filler words, make sure you take special care to eliminate this prose mistake.

3. Summarize Each Chapter in One or Two Sentences

This is a quick study to help you find if your plot flow makes logical sense. It'll also help you get a feel for your novel as you try to revise it in the future. You need to know every chapter, paragraph, sentence and word where it's placed like a chess mastermind. Some say this is the editor's job, but who knows the story better than the person who wrote it? Truly know your novel inside and out. When you are intimate with the structure of your novel, you will be able to find plot holes and character actions/reactions that just don't make logical sense. You'll likely even discover entire scenes that don't move the plot along and need to be cut. It's a simple exercise with large rewards.

Some people say that it takes too much time to do such revision techniques as I've mentioned here. That's why they hire expensive editors to do it for them. But honestly, if you had enough time to write the novel, why don't you have enough time to make it publishable? A first draft is a very long set of musings, a first revision is your high school homework project, and maybe a few revisions after that is an actual publishable piece of work, depending on your skill at editing and those assisting you.

3 Drafts to a Publishable Manuscript

Are you pursuing traditional publishing? Do you feel your manuscript is ready to be put in front of an editor or agent? Go through this list before you do! (If self-publishing, further recommendations are at the end of this section.)

According to Literary Agent Paula Munier in her book "Writing With Quiet Hands," there are three major drafts before you arrive at a publishable novel. I know I bring up this resource a lot, but it's seriously worth the read.

First Draft: Write whatever you wish to write, be it from a carefully constructed outline or by the seat of your pants. Don't worry about the words, just get them down on paper. You can make it pretty later.

Second Draft: Before starting the second draft, there are two things you may want to consider first. Beta readers and putting your draft down for a while so you can get some distance. (Conveniently, it takes beta readers a few weeks to go through a book so two birds with one stone!)

Using your feedback, sit down and do a "big picture" edit. Some hire a developmental editor for this kind of edit, which is NOT the same as a line edit. That's for the third draft.

A *big picture edit should include:

• You have a likable protagonist.

• The main character leads the plot by their choices and isn't a passive character where the plot just seems to "happen" to them.

• Plot Arc with a clear beginning, middle, and end. A logical sequence of events that seamlessly lead from one plot point to the next. If you didn't write an outline for your story, you should write one now to properly analyze your plot flow.

• Sub-Plot arcs are present and add to the story.

• Logical and completed character arcs: The main character is trying to fix a problem and only seems to make it worse, encountering obstacles, good intentions gone wrong hinder your main character along the way until they finally get what they're after, and have grown as a character at the same time. All antagonists are relatable, and even if we hate them, we can still empathize with their actions.

○   Truly understanding your characters will help if when you do a rewrite. You'll be able to write with more conviction, and perhaps find a sense of voice you had been missing because you honestly didn't really know the rooted motivations of why your characters did what they did, and what they wanted out of life.

• Narrative Thrust: The reader is constantly asking questions that will lead to the next plot point, which is essential to keeping their interest. Paula has a large chapter dedicated to this concept as well as a guest blog post, and I can't stress its importance enough. (I have no affiliation with Jane Friedman's blog, I'm just one of her many readers.)

• Every character and scene has a purpose and serves to develop the story.

• There is a healthy balance of Character, Description, Backstory, Setting, and Conflict. (Meaning no info-dumps, and no superfluous information.)

Have you done a REAL Second Draft?

Remember, you're not answering me, you're answering yourself. You need to sit down and think long and hard and ask yourself, have I done everything possible to do a proper second draft?

If you are squirming in your chair and going b-b-but... don't shy away from it! This is a good thing. There's actually something YOU can do in order to make your book more attractive to agents. Isn't that awesome? If you saw an advertisement that said "Guaranteed product to make your manuscript more attractive to agents," wouldn't you buy it? It isn't a secret, you will meet your goals if you want it bad enough, and that comes with putting the work into understanding your story down to its core and revising until it's right.

This doesn't mean you have to go hire a developmental editor, and I wouldn't recommend it anyway unless you have reliable writer friends who can give proper recommendations. There are freelance editors out there who don't really know what they're doing, and you have to learn how to edit your own work anyway!

Buy some books written by respectable authors/editors/agents, join a writers' critique group, read recent debut novels that broke into your genre and study what about them you can emulate-- in short, commit yourself to the craft. If you want to meet your goals, that's how it's going to happen. Believe in yourself and what you're capable of, you're stronger than you realize.

Third Draft: This is the "icing on the cake" draft and the last edit you do before you submit your work.

You've done everything you can to make the nitty-gritty content of your novel the best it can possibly be. You have an awesome, likable main character, you have a villain we love to hate, and you've got a premise that is skillfully executed.

Now you need to do a line edit, and this is what really makes your novel shine. How much effort you spend on this draft is the equivalent of how much a jeweler polishes his gems. Don't hand over your novel with grime and grit caked on it to an agent, not when you know it's an uncut diamond not ready to be set in a ring. Take your time and weed out all unnecessary words, and achieve a review that labels your prose as "crisp" and "elegant." Read your novel out loud, and any place you find yourself tripping means you've got a sentence you need to either reword, or cut altogether. If it doesn't work, don't stress over it. Sometimes it's easier to delete than to repair.

I think a big mistake novelists make is heading straight into the third draft. When s/he realizes the novel didn't have a proper second draft, things need to be rewritten, and now s/he has completely wasted their time icing a cake that wasn't yet baked. Don't be impatient! Give your novel the second draft it deserves and you'll find your novel is much better received when it's time to pitch it to an agent.

This is my take of a "big picture edit" based on my study of "Writing With Quiet Hands," and is not a copy/paste of the book's content. That said, this section is a brief summary of the large extent Paula goes into of what a big picture edit really means, and how to do one. I suggest reading her novel if you would like to be inspired to write, pick up tips, and good writing habits from someone who knows.

CRITIQUE
GROUPS
&
BETA
READERS

CHAPTER SEVEN

Critique Groups and Beta Readers

3 Reasons Critiquing Can Improve Your Writing

There you are, sitting with your morning coffee, a warming laptop and a small journal of jumbled notes. After you finish your first draft and begin the revising process, you keep finding the same mistakes over and over again... Why does this keep happening?

I think this is a common problem most writers have to endure. When writing the draft, you can't just "pre-edit." You let the words come out...adverbs, misused commas and repetitions galore.

We are all on a quest to improve our writing. But do you know one of the best ways you can improve your writing? Stop looking at your own work and try to edit someone else's. Wait, did I read that correctly? Yes! Go edit someone else's work.

Why? I'm so glad you asked.

1. You are not emotionally attached.

The best thing about looking at work you didn't write is that you are not in-love with it. You didn't birth it from your heart and soul, so it's free game to tear it to shreds. When you are in this state of mind, you can easily find parallels to your own work.

For example, you just heartlessly cut out two paragraphs of info-dump. You aggressively type: "Completely irrelevant! Cut it all!" Then you gasp. You did the very same thing in your own first Chapter! Time to look in the mirror.

2. Others will have different strengths and weaknesses than you.

It's one thing to go read a book by a pro, and by all means I recommend that you constantly read anything published by respected sources. But it's entirely another to read a fellow aspiring writer's work. They will have unique strengths that are a golden opportunity to teach something you didn't know.

For example, one of my writing weaknesses is trying to write dialogue scenes. My poor characters repeat the same gestures, there's a whole lot of sighing, glances and winces. I've recently come across a fellow writer that lacks clarity, but their dialogue scenes are stellar. I've learned a whole new array of ways to express gestures to accentuate dialogue. Without the careful, analytical eye I am putting to a piece like this, I likely never would have picked up that tidbit in a published work.

3. You become exposed to undiluted voice.

In published works, there are plenty of varieties in voice. But I want to reiterate that critiquing a work puts one in a whole different mindset. You are in "analysis" mode, not reading for enjoyment. You will find yourself nodding your head or shaking it. You take everything in with a critical eye. And when a stylistic voice pops out at you and impresses you, that's when you know that it's something to examine for yourself. Out of all the grammar mistakes, the info-dump and bumbling scenes there was a voice that touched you? What about it was so powerful to overcome the flaws of the raw piece?

It's easy for a published work to have beautiful voice, because that work has been edited down to its bones. Not to say that those authors aren't talented or gifted, I'm sure they are. But it's in a raw draft and unedited piece that still has a voice that really shows color and vision. I have found a few gems such as this and learned a handful of skills to take with me to my own creative world.

So with that, I encourage you to go yonder and help others! They don't have to know your selfish motives. Mum's the word.

Should I Utilize Beta Readers?

After finishing my first novel "Fallen to Grace" two years ago, I spent a large portion of my free time editing and revising. I've gotten a lot of constructive critique feedback. From this I've been able to improve the glaring flaws and sneaky typos.

I'll admit, I've taken my sweet time with my first novel. It's the beauty of being an unpublished author. But now I'm ready to take this seriously, it's time to stop dragging my feet. Two months ago I took my efforts up a notch and started spitting out query letters and ramping up beta readers. Nothing is going to stop me from getting my work published. I'm ready.

As it stands now, I'm happy with my manuscript. I feel it's perfectly ready for the world. However, after a few beta reads I'm left hopelessly confused. I wonder if all writers go through this? Was it a mistake to even have beta readers?

The general feedback is:
50% - Wow! Your writing technique is so eloquent, you have some sick talent. This is beautiful.
50% - ... You seriously expect to publish this? The story is awesome, but the storytelling has me bored.

This is the first time I've gone through beta readers, and I think if I went through more I'm going to get the same result. It would make sense, in the world of entertainment there is nothing that everyone loves. But I was hoping for something more helpful than 50-50.
Considering other published works, there are different levels of fame.

1) You have the popular fads, but those fade quickly. And only the selective targeted audience is going to love it.

2) The old classics, which are classic for a reason: they have a unique quality that stands them apart from everything else.

3) And there are definitely those works that are a love/hate relationship. Either you love it, or you just can't stand it.
Maybe I have to accept that my debut novel is in the third category.

I'm going to look at this as a "glass-half-full" situation and keep trudging on. J.K. Rowling took ~200 queries to find an agent, if I hit that mark without success then I will consider rewriting my voice. Or otherwise, pursue self-publishing (half an audience isn't half-bad). I know my second manuscript doesn't have this issue, from the feedback I've received Sanctuary is closer to 80%-Like 20%-Not a Fan.

In the meantime, I will consider the feedback from the 50% haters on Fallen to Grace, but honestly if I take such advice I will be rewriting the entire voice of my manuscript. In the end, I have to decide on giving in, and risk losing the 50% which do like my work as it is, or stick to my gut which tells me to keep my novel genuine to me.

To answer the section question: Should I have my novel beta read? Yes.

Even though I personally got such conflicting results, I still think the answer is yes. Even with information overload, or conflicting information, it's important to judge how the public will react to your work. I'm happier knowing rather than not. Instead of frolicking in the fields of "I'm awesome," I'm forced to sit down and seriously ponder my work. My final decision will be an informed one.

What Beta Readers Mean by Pacing Problems

I've run into an interesting problem with my beta readers that's baffled me for weeks. Pacing. Every single one of them said my first chapter's pace was just too slow. But that didn't make much sense to me. I have prose scuffed down to a satisfying crisp. I had a sequence of events moved by the main character. I had a hook and a page-turner, everything a Chapter 1 was supposed to have. Sure, some people noticed the work I put into it, how beautifully crafted it was, even said "wow!" but then the pacing complaint came soon thereafter. Why?

Then I decoded the beta-speak. It wasn't a pacing problem, it was an *urgency* problem.

Let me explain what I mean by urgency. My main character was in danger, but it was a "possible" danger. He's hiding, and if he's caught he could die. You know what would be better? If he were being *chased.* Then it is an "immediate" and "urgent" problem. The reader has to jump to action NOW and flee the scene, rather than scratch their nose and wonder what might happen if they step out of the shadows.

Passage A: Example of a present but not immediate danger:

Henry grasped the stolen fruit, desperately wishing he could shove it into his mouth. But if he did, the merchant would hear him. And if he left his cubby in the wall, he'd certainly be apprehended. Henry didn't move a muscle, and waited for the merchant to leave.

Passage B: Example of an immediate danger:

Henry clutched the stolen fruit to his chest like a football as he ran. The merchant roared behind him flailing a knife that glinted against the sun. Henry's heart jumped in his throat and his feet flew like the wind, taking him to the one place he knew he'd be safe: the graveyard.

This is just a quick example I wrote for the purposes of this book, and I think it illustrates the point I'm trying to make. Passage A may be interesting, but it's a dull and slow kind of interesting. Then Passage B comes along, and we're launched into the ride, ready and excited to see what's going to come next.

So consider what your beta readers are saying the next time they complain of slow pace. It just may be that your action isn't present and immediate, and that's the change you need to focus on.

SELF-
PUBLISHING

CHAPTER EIGHT

Self-Publishing

Is Self-Publishing the New Norm?

Self-publishing has become increasingly popular. At first, I imagined it was because of how difficult it is to get through the slush pile. But the more I learn, the more I realize there is much more than that to consider. There are some strong points that make self-publishing very attractive. So attractive in fact, that some authors have even turned away from traditional publishing to pursue self-publishing, even when given the choice.

Here are my thoughts on why:

• Less people are involved in the process, meaning more profit can go to the author.

Traditional: 6-15% to the author

Self: 35% up to a whopping 70% to the author - 35% will be more common and give you freedoms that a larger royalty will not

There is a lot of fine print associated with those numbers, but you can get the general idea. If you can market your work well, which you will need to do regardless of which route you take, self-publishing may be more profitable.

• Self-Publishing is fast. From acceptance - to the publisher - to on the shelf, is an average of one to two years, assuming there are no hiccups. Self-publishing is on your own time-table. Book is edited, formatted, and ready to go with a cover? Hit the button. This a very attractive bit of self-publishing that many authors appreciate. Although I am sure many impatient authors make the mistake of hitting the publish button too soon, and the result is an unfinished product that gathers dust in the corner.

• Control is given to the author. I find this one very important. When considering a publisher, the author has little to no choice in the cover, marketing process, giveaways, and sometimes even the book sub-plots. How much will a publisher force you to revise your work to match marketing statistics or make sure we're all politically correct? Self-publishing means you don't have to answer to anyone but yourself. But beware, with great power comes great responsibility. (Sorry, couldn't help myself there.)

All in all, there is a lot to consider for which route is best for you. There are many award-winning authors that have started out by self-publishing, and eventually signed million dollar contracts with publishers after their wild success. (For example, Andy Weir who wrote "The Martian," now a Twentieth Century Fox Motion Picture.) Of course, very few make it this big. Keep your expectations realistic.

On the flip-side, traditional publishing has a sense of "hitting it big", though do not confuse that with big money. It means you are pre-vetted and approved by the "big-boys". Even though it could be argued that even self-published works are separated by hefty reviews and best-seller spotlights, there's a sense of accomplishment, recognition and success attributed to becoming published by a big name. But depending on your goals, that may or may not matter to you.

All authors need to sit back and really consider which route that works best for them. Times are changing, and it is becoming easier to be an Indie-Author than it ever has before.

Do Judge a Book By Its Cover

As I said before, writing a good book is only half the battle. The other half is full of a lot of things that have very little to do with writing. Having the proper cover is one of them!

You're somewhere in-between elementary school and middle school when you learn an important English idiom: *Never Judge a Book by its Cover*. Perhaps this wisdom was departed by a grey-haired woman, parroted by a well-meaning classmate, or an all-knowing parent. You widen your eyes and nod emphatically. Of course, I should never judge a book by its cover!

While this idiom may hold true in a metaphorical sense, I am jumping on the controversial wagon of disagreement for its literal message. I DO judge a book by its cover, and I think you should too.

Maybe once-upon-a-time, this idiom held some literal truth. I imagine it was hard enough to get inks and paper, much less reproduce creative works of art for each book distributed. But now in the modern age this is not such an obstacle. There is absolutely no reason an author/publisher should not have an astounding & fantastic cover for a new release novel. Think about it, the author has put months, or even years, into this work. It's their baby, their heart and soul. Why on earth would someone go through so much blood, sweat and tears and not invest the same into the one image that will display that work to the world? There is no excuse, and it's an insult to good literature.

I'll give a parental comparison here: My mother did not dress me up in a potato sack skirt and shove me down the street. No, she dressed me up in a frilly white dress and put red ribbons in my hair. She was proud of me, and let the world know it!

A decent cover will run an author/publisher $0-$1,000. Of course, it depends who you know, or if you have some stellar art skills yourself. But even if money is an issue and your creative well has run dry, there are plenty of new artists out there that are looking for some credit. It will take some elbow-rubbing and effort to search out the right cover, but that's effort well spent, isn't it?

When I'm searching for a new novel, I normally go first by word-of-mouth. But when I am browsing Amazon pages or wandering the aisles of Barnes & Noble, there is only one thing that's going to make me reach out and grab or click that book. The cover has grabbed my attention. If I see an epic battle scene of elves with swords and flying arrows, I guarantee I'm going to pick up that book and check it out. Because I get an immediate impression there is some awesome battle scene in there that I'm going to want to be a part of. And likewise, the author has done their best to represent their work in a properly marketable fashion, they put in the effort that says they care about their work.

If I see a poorly drawn flower, a lopsided character's face or otherwise boring cover on excessively-cheap paperback, I likely won't pick it up. The author/publisher did not put in any effort, so why should I?

Now, for you readers who are shouting, BUT! "Such-and-Such" was FABULOUS, and it has a HIDEOUS cover. Yes, I'm sure there are plenty exceptions to this generalization I'm making. But likely that author either 1) did not care about their work enough to sport a decent cover, 2) were too inexperienced to take the time to look at the options 3) has enough awards under their belt that they can do whatever they want.

No, as book-purchasing members of society, we deserve better than that.

3 Resources for you Cover

So you're self-publishing, and you're ready for an awesome cover. I've always been a staunch supporter of the best images authors can possibly manage to showcase themselves. And while important, writers will quickly find how expensive and challenging it can be to find a decent cover.

I'll give you an example of my one of my flash fiction story's cover photo:

The image is a royalty-free CC0 License image from Pixabay and the template I used was from Canva Cover maker. By the end of this section you'll know what all that means!

This cover was completely free minus the work I put into it. I can't use expensive covers for every flash fiction I write, so this is a great alternative while keeping the quality of my showcase at a level I can be proud of and allow me to allocate funds for editing services and cover photos of self-published works.

So, are you ready to build up your showcase? Let's get started.

To make a cover or display for your blog post, you'll first need an awesome image. Without the image, you won't have much to work with!

1) Free resources:

If you try searching for quality images exclusively for your own use, or even customized, it's going to get expensive, and fast. Until you're rich and famous (snickers), I'm going to assume you don't have thousands of dollars to spend on images.

What you need are stock images. A stock image is a supply of images with a specific license, and the one you're looking for is going to be "**creative commons zero**" or (**CC0**). Be careful not to confuse this with a regular Creative Commons image, which without the zero means you still need to give credit to the creator. However, CC0 means the image is allowed to be used for any purpose and you don't need to give credit.

There are many different licenses and range from how much credit you must give, what kind of edits you're allowed to do on the image (if at all), and what purpose you may use the image for. Be sure to understand what license an image has, and if a license is not listed, you should assume you cannot use that image without first speaking to the creator.

If you're unsure who the creator is, you can try sourcing sites like "TinEye" to locate where the image is from. But ultimately, the safest way to make sure you know the license and true creator of an image is to use a website designed for this purpose.

The downside with a stock image is that it's not exclusive, and it can be difficult to find what you're looking for that's also a high-quality image. The upside is that most of the general public has probably not seen the image before, and it is a free resource to get you started in your ventures.

(If you would like clickable links to easily find these resources, please download the Kindle version of this guide.)

Resources:

(Free if you have Kindle Unlimited) Amazon High-Quality Photo Collections: The Stock Photo Book: Images include landscapes, seascapes, wildlife, macro, and a few with people.
The Royalty Free Images Book: Mostly dogs & cats as well as landscapes.
The Royalty Free Photo Collection: Focus on Pets and Landscapes.
Book Cover Design Market Research:
4.4/5 stars rated Market Research Book: Book Cover Design Secrets You Can Use to Sell More Books, Free with Kindle Unlimited
"Book Marketing Bible" : An excellent resource if you really don't know where to start. The Cover is just the start of getting your book out there. Free with Kindle Unlimited.

Free Image Websites:

FreeImages.com: A large resource, just be sure to adjust your search parameters for free images. Not all will be great quality, but they're in there. I mostly use this site for blog post images.
Pixabay (my personal favorite): Beautiful images and a nice selection. I've had success using this site for images suitable for fantasy more than others.
PicJumbo: Ironically, their selection isn't exactly "Jumbo" but the quality of these free images cannot be denied.
SkitterPhoto: Beautiful and Creative Images, and they're free. (Mostly Nature, Cities, and Random Photo Shots-- but well done.)
Gratisography: Artsy   and   Whimsical   High-Quality Photos with Landscapes/Nature/People

Websites with daily/weekly free images or sign-up required collections:
Unsplash: Mostly landscapes, but the images are breathtaking. Requires sign-up.
IM Free: Small Library but high quality photos.

I want to mention I don't recommend using Google to search for images. Even though you can go into the advanced search options (Search Tools -> Usage Rights -> Labeled for Reuse) it doesn't mean you'll find only CCO images. Many images that pop up are still controlled by the creator and you will need to verify what kind of credit and purposes you may use the image for.

You may want a map for your fantasy world, and in this case check out this helpful tutorial to make one yourself. Or if you're not so creatively inclined, there is software designed to help you create one: a nice list is on this Reddit post.

2) Paid Resources:

If free resources don't have what you're looking for, you could consider purchasing images. Depending on the type of license you need, paid images can range from under a dollar to 100$, though the common price for an emerging writer's needs would be around $15 per image. Rest assured, it only gets expensive when you're looking for a marketing image to sell over 500,000 copies. Unless you're a massive best-seller, I don't think you'll need to worry about selling more copies than that (and if you do, you can afford to hire whatever artist you want.) But if you just love the stock image, and you pass 500,000 sold copies, then you'd need an extended license which has a price range of roughly 100$ to 500$.

Shutterstock (one of my favorites, images are around 15$ each): Shutterstock has a large selection and I've had the most success finding images suitable for book covers on this site.
DepositPhotos: I don't like their selection as much but they are a little cheaper, ranging from 40 cents to 15$ per image.
iStockPhoto: Decent selection but they run on a "Credit" system. You can purchase credits which are then used to purchase photos. I don't usually like it when a merchant makes their own currency, but if you plan on purchasing a lot of photos this can save you money in the long run.
GhettyImages: I haven't had much luck with this site since images are expensive (~50$+) and more suited for freelance work than fantasy covers. However it is still a good resource so I'm including it for reference.

3) Hire a Professional:

The last stage would be to find your own artist to make an image or cover for you. Here are some resources, but I recommend you simply do your homework and investigate cover artists and compare their portfolios and pricing, as well as reviews from past customers. Expect to pay anywhere from $500 to $2,000 for your cover. However, keep an eye out for emerging artists. They may be willing to give you a discount or do your cover for free as long as you provide them credit to help them build their portfolio.

Resources to find cover artists:
GoodReads Forum where posts are made to suggest illustrators

DeviantArt is a go-to for artists. Peruse and find work you like, then reach out to the artist.

Reedsy is a popular resource for Editors and Book Designers. I feel a little more comfortable with this website because it's a professional site with a resume-like listing, including past experiences and client reviews.

AUTHOR
INTERVIEWS

CHAPTER NINE

Author Interviews

Introduction

This section is a short list of author interviews I've held over 2014. These are everyday writers to give you a good idea of what to expect. What I like is you can see that every writer goes through great hardship to get their writing out into the world, and you're not alone. Other than that, it's a great opportunity to pick someone's brain about what worked for them, and what didn't. I hope you find these interviews as useful as I did.

Luke Brimblecombe

Luke Brimblecombe has self-published the psychological thriller "Zero Anaphora" as an e-book and softcover (2014).

Tell us a little about yourself. What got you into writing?

I wrote a short novel back in 2001 in the holidays between graduating from high-school and going to university the next year. I tried again in 2004. My writing was really bad back then, but I was inspired by how much it improved each time I found the inspiration for a new project. Life experience, reading, and using language in general still does enough to improve you though. New writers shouldn't have their hopes set too high for the results of their first attempt.

How did you come up with your story?

It's a gradual process of starting with a central premise and building up around it systematically. It's also good to work with other people when developing your plot ideas, especially if you like to plan your structures in advance.

Tell me about your experience, what were the biggest challenges and how did you overcome them?

The biggest challenge was disinterest from friends and family. People love the idea that you are working on a book, but when presented with an unfinished, digital document, you apparently can't expect them to spend much of their own time on it. Fair enough too!

What is the result? Are you doing well? What would you have done differently if you could do it all again?

The result is that I'm improving as a writer and finding the process of creating literature to be quite a fulfilling and rewarding activity. I prefer to set performance oriented goals rather than results oriented ones. That means looking forward to changing a certain aspect of my text for the better, NOT seeing a certain number of copies of it on a bookshelf.

What are you working on now? What are your future plans?

I'm going to write a series of fantasy e-books for self publishing, the first will be free. It's going really well, I'm collaborating with a friend who helps me develop the ideas quite a bit when we get together for workshop sessions.

What advice would you give unpublished writers?

Focus on improving your technical ability and mental approach. You need to be actively looking for people who are capable of giving you genuine feedback about what is wrong with your writing. Don't set out to 'get published' unless you are already well-known for having stories published in magazines, or you've done newspaper columns/articles, or unless you're already famous for something.

Just for fun, which character would you kill off in your book if you had to and why?

All my characters are expendable, but I would prefer to make the death of a character as relevant to the plot as possible.

Let's hear about your Self-Publishing endeavor. Did you hire an Editor to revise your work? If not, do you regret it?

No, it's not worth hiring someone to do that when you can get the same result by working very hard on the text yourself, and also working hard to get others to read through the text before you go public with it.

Was it difficult finding the right cover and blurb?

Yes, but I ended up hiring a cover-creator, and following the recommendations of an indie-reviews site for blurb creation. I was by no means happy with either.

What made you decide to go the self-publishing route?

I self-published because I wanted it published, for a sense of self-satisfaction, and the opportunity to promote myself as a writer for future projects. It would have been a waste of time to try to get published traditionally.

Mandy Webster

Mandy has written and self-published a Middle Grade Novel: "Young Marian A Viper in the Forest" available in paperback or Kindle eBook. A delightful spin on Robin Hood in a world encased by English Folklore.

Amazon 5-Star Reviews:

"beautiful use of language" - Louisa M

"A refreshing change to see Marian as the main character" - Mike W.

"I found it difficult to put down" - Colleen Cronin

"I highly recommend it for any young girl, mother of a young girl, or anyone with a love for a good story!" - JAS

"exciting, with lots of action and drama, and the characters are very well drawn out" - Elaine C. Reid

Tell us a little about yourself. What got you into writing?

Although I always enjoyed writing, I started out in design. I was working in the production department of a magazine when I approached the editor and asked if I could try my hand at writing an article. As soon as I saw my first piece in print I had the bug! I began writing more at the magazine and then moved from there to copywriting at an advertising agency.

After staying home to raise my kids for a few years, I returned to work as a writer for a popular children's website. I would spend all day writing stories for children and it was heaven. It helps that I am a big kid myself – I've read Harry Potter countless times and I'm usually the one dragging my kids to Disney movies and theme parks.

How did you come up with your story?

When I was a teenager we moved from Canada to a tiny village in the English countryside. It was idyllic. I've always loved history, romance and adventure books, so folk tales like Robin Hood and King Arthur completely enthralled me. My favorite TV show at the time was Robin of Sherwood, and 20 years later I fell in love the new BBC version of Robin Hood too.

I took some time off work and had been thinking about writing a book for a while. I'd read a couple of the Young James Bond books and was aware of the Young Sherlock Holmes (another of my favorite TV shows was the short-lived 'Young Indiana Jones' in the 90's). I started thinking about telling the story of Robin Hood before he became the outlaw we all know so well.

While I had always planned for Marian to be a kickass character who could hold her own with the boys, it occurred to me that a great twist on the tale would be to make Marian the hero of the story.

And so it became a new take on a classic legend in which the girl takes the lead and the boys are the secondary characters.

Tell me about your experience, what were the biggest challenges and how did you overcome them?

By far my biggest challenge is self-discipline and actually forcing myself to sit down and write. I kept waiting for the day that I would wake up and think to myself 'Today's the day!' but it never came.

One day I was watching Conan O'Brien being interviewed about the process of making his show and how hard it is. He said something along the lines of

'If someone says they love writing, I don't want to read anything they wrote.' That was a wakeup call to me. Writing is a discipline - if I kept waiting for the day I really WANTED to write I could be waiting forever.

I also hate and dread self-promotion. It's funny because I work in marketing, and I have no issues with singing the praises of my company in our ads, but when it comes to saying anything good about myself I get extremely uncomfortable. The day I actually put myself out there and asked my friends to 'like' my Facebook page was one of the most difficult days in the entire process!

I think that trait is one a lot of women share, not wanting to blow our own horns. I guess I need to take a page out of Marian's book (no pun intended!) - recognize my strengths and refuse to let anything stand in my way!

What is the result? Are you doing well? What would you have done differently if you could do it all again?

Well, when my book hit #1 in its category on Amazon.ca I was thrilled! It also reached #25 on Amazon.com, which was pretty cool. But as far as sales go, I am completely realistic about the fact that I have to look at the long term. I am focused on the future - laying the groundwork for the rest of the series. Right now I consider any sale over and above the one I bought myself a huge success!

If I could have done anything differently, I would have started workshopping my chapters with other writers earlier. I wrote the first four chapters and then stalled for about six months because I knew I needed feedback, but I didn't know where to find it. Then I discovered a wonderful writing community that has helped me immensely. Not only was the feedback essential but some days when I was having a hard time finding inspiration, receiving an encouraging review of my work was just what I needed to get me back on track.

What are you working on now? What are your future plans?

'A Viper in the Forest' is the first in the Young Marian series. I am currently working on book two and book three is floating around in the back of my mind. My goal is to release one book a year for the next five or six years. After that, my Marian and Robin tale will catch up with the existing legends and it will be time for me to move on. I would love to develop a new story with original characters. Whatever I do, I see myself continuing to write for children or maybe young adults. My first book sort of straddles the line between MG and YA.

What advice would you give unpublished writers?

First of all, make time for writing and then actually do it! That was the biggest hurdle for me.

Secondly, seek out other writers and get as much feedback as you can. This has made the biggest difference to my writing. There are wonderful online communities, or local writers' groups. Friends and family are great, but they have a tendency to tell us what we want to hear. What a writer really needs is constructive criticism from objective readers who share their passion for the written word and aren't afraid to be honest.

Just for fun, which character would you kill off in your book if you had to and why?

Well, unfortunately one particularly unpleasant character, Ranulf has a role to play in the next book, but if I didn't need him alive I would happily smite him!

Let's hear about your Self-Publishing endeavor. Did you hire an Editor to revise your work?

I wish I had the budget to have hired an editor but as completing this book was really fulfilling a fantasy of mine, I just couldn't justify the cost.

Having said that, I found the input from peers in my workshopping group to be absolutely invaluable. They pick up on little things, like typos and punctuation, and they also notice the big things, like plot holes I may have completely missed.

I had a couple of beta readers and my father-in-law is a successful published author so he read it and made some excellent suggestions. My sister is an amazing proofreader and she was the final set of eyes.

Was it difficult finding the right cover and blurb?

Well, I have a graphic design background so I was able to do my own cover. I had been thinking of a more traditional look using photography, but one day I had an inspiration that I wanted something unique yet simple. I laid it out fairly quickly and it just seemed right. Other than a few tweaks here and there it hasn't really changed from that first iteration.

My cover may have a slightly more mature feel than some middle grade books, but the book is directed at older kids – 10 to14 – so I thought it would appeal to their sensibilities.

I worked with a strategist who helped me with the Amazon description and my author bio. Of course, the writer in me wants to second guess every word someone else writes – especially when it's about ME! But she has worked in publishing for years. She knew the tricks to formatting it so that it really tells the reader who the book is for and what the benefits are to them. There's a lot more to it than I realized – I'm so glad I had her help.

What made you decide to go the self-publishing route?

A few years ago I attempted the traditional route with a picture book I had written and it never went anywhere. I do realize that picture books are a hard sell, but this time around I just decided I would skip the long, uphill battle that, statistically speaking, would probably end in more rejections. Rather than spinning my wheels for a couple of years with nothing to show for it, I decided just to get my story out there.

I also knew I had the resources to execute it fairly economically as well as making it look professional and polished. And of course Amazon and Createspace make the whole process pretty painless.

Connect with Mandy Webster:

Twitter: @MandyWebster
Facebook: https://www.facebook.com/youngmarianbook
Website: www.youngmarian.com

Elizabeth Davies

Elizabeth Davies has written and self-published 5 full-length novels. Her latest being "The Medium Path," a paranormal romance with a fascinating premise.

Amazon 5-star Reviews of "The Medium Path":

"The Medium Path is an intriguing read that will capture your imagination and your heart" - Amy Valentini

"A fabulous, engaging ghostly tale! Love this author!" - Carmen

"Elizabeth Davies is a gifted storyteller. She never disappoints" Carmie Lee
Tell us a little about yourself. What got you into writing?

Reading has been my passion for as long as I can remember. I was always to be found with a book in my hand, content to lose myself in a story. I never thought I'd write one myself. But one day I was chatting to a friend about how I would love go back to 18 years old and live my life over again, with the benefit of the knowledge and experiences I have now. An idea for a novel was born. It will never see the light of day, but having completed one story, I knew I could write another.

How did you come up with your story?

The first novel I self-published was called State of Grace, and is about a woman who travels back in time and discovers vampires really do exist. This rather strange mix comes from watching too much True Blood and getting hooked on vampires, and wanting to combine in with my love of medieval history.

Tell me about your experience, what were the biggest challenges and how did you overcome them?

Self-published was a very steep learning curve for me. The biggest challenge was not to write the novel itself, but the editing, publishing, marketing process. I had no money to commission a set of three covers (I had three books in mind for the series) and none of the pre-made out there at the time were close enough in theme, model,etc to link together. So I did my own, and not very well either. Realising a writer can't catch all their own typos etc, was another thing I wasn't expecting. The only solution to this is to hire a proofreader.

What is the result? Are you doing well? What would you have done differently if you could do it all again?

For an unknown writer I'm doing okay. I don't make enough to give up my regular job and any royalties goes towards the next edit, the next book cover. If I could do it again, I would join a writers group first. I found the critiques invaluable in improving my writing.

What are you working on now? What are your future plans?

I stated work on another paranormal romance concerting a witch's familiar. The first draft is almost done and I was hoping to publish for Halloween -

until a friend pointed out that this novel should actually be the last in a series. When I thought about it, I realised she was right! So now I've got myself a series. A number of readers have also asked if I plan to write another book about Grace. (Resurrection series)I did intend the last one to be the last one, but then an idea for another Grace story popped into my head, and it just won't go away!

What advice would you give unpublished writers?

Keep writing. Perfect your craft. Join a writing circle/group. Beta read - it will make you a better writer (honest). Make friends with other authors - most writers are more than happy to give advice. Keep writing. I know I said that twice but without practice your writing won't improve. Don't complete a manuscript and sit back and wait for responses from agents/publishers - you may have a long wait, so work on your next project.

Just for fun, which character would you kill off in your book if you had to and why?

Roman from the Resurrection series. My readers would be horrified!

Let's hear about your Self-Publishing endeavor. Did you hire an Editor to revise your work?

Not at first. I put my first novel out there 'littered with mistakes' as one reviewer quite accurately pointed out. And I certainly did regret it. Lesson learned!

Was it difficult finding the right cover and blurb?

I can lose hours scrolling through pre-made book covers and stock photos looking for ideas. It's a real problem for me. I can't resist - even though I know I'm going to ask Nicole Spence from Cover Shot Creations to work her magic. And when she emails me a proof I still um and ah, in spite of the fact I know it's perfect.

Blurbs? Ha! Don't even go there. I know what doesn't work for me when I read other people's blurbs, but getting it right for my own is a whole different issue. Still don't think I've nailed it...

What made you decide to go the self-publishing route?

No one would take me on! I approached numerous agents and all said 'thanks, but no thanks'. They may well have had a point - when I read back *through my earliest work I cringe. Now I am happy with being self-published. I've got all the control, and I like that.*

Connect with Elizabeth Davies:

website: http://www.elizabethdaviesauthor.co.uk
blog: http://elizabethdaviesbooks.blogspot.co.uk
Twitter : @bethsbooks

Emma Woods

Emma Woods has self-published her debut YA fiction novel: "Beasts and Savages."

Tell us a little about yourself. What got you into writing?

I'm a small town, Midwestern girl with no big story. I've always loved reading and writing, and was sure I'd grow up to be a teacher. So did everyone else. I have the teaching degree, but not the job. In a way, I'm glad it worked out like that. If I were a teacher, I don't know if I would have gone back to writing as an adult. As a child, I read anything I could get my hands on and couldn't wait every year for Young Author events. I got back into writing as an adult when I began to make a children's book series called Sun and Moon for my daughter to illustrate. Something just for fun.

How did you come up with your story?

Tumblr. Someone had a post about not wanting another YA story about a girl who changes her entire life for a boy she falls for at the moment they meet. Someone else made a comment about a girl seeing a boy for the first time "and there he was, the first boy I'm going to kill..." People commented about how they'd love to read a story like that, so I wrote one. I even messaged the original blogger to thank him for the idea. I got no response, so I guess he isn't interested.

Tell me about your experience, what were the biggest challenges and how did you overcome them?

My experience was probably much different than most. I told a friend about my writing after she asked me what I was doing while our kids were at swim practice, and she encouraged me to write the novel and post it on Smashwords. I had been emailing my sister each chapter, she whole heartedly agreed, and has been a huge supporter ever since. My sister, Wendy, has been my partner in crime when it comes to help with social media, marketing, scene suggestions, and she even formatted my eBooks for me.

My biggest challenge, by far, has been how little I knew about becoming, and being, an indie author. I started writing in March, joined an editing group in July, and thought I'd have a book ready by August, September at the latest. I was wrong, and even after my book launched, I wasn't ready. Not really ready, and every day I learn about something else that I could be doing.

What is the result? Are you doing well? What would you have done differently if you could do it all again?

For a "newbie", I feel like I'm doing okay in some aspects, and not in others. I have lots of local support and I can't keep my cash and carry paperbacks in stock. Am I a best seller? Not even close. What I'm lacking is reviews. I didn't even realize how important reviews were until a week after I published. If I had it to do over again, I'd delay announcing a publishing date until I was sure the book was finished and I had some advanced reviews under my belt.

What are you working on now? What are your future plans?

I'm working on the second book in The Beastly Series, which I don't have a full title for just yet. I plan to finish it during Nanowrimo and release it on April 1, 2016. I want to finish the three book series by the end of 2016, and after that I have some companion books in mind. Beyond that, who knows? I have so many ideas in the back of my mind.

What advice would you give unpublished writers?

Write for you. I know this has been said before, but it bears repeating. Write a story because you love it. If you miss typos in your own story because you got sucked in, then you're doing everything right. Also, never self-edit, and don't be afraid to throw out sentences, scenes, or entire chapters. Nine times out of ten, if someone tells me to chuck something out, it's gone, or at least shortened.

Just for fun, do you have any writing quirks you'd care to share?

I talk aloud to myself while I write. I'll say things like, "What if Lea told Miller she didn't want to hear his sob story? Nah, Lea's not like that." I think my dog finds it amusing, or a little disturbing, I'm not sure which. ;)

Let's hear about your Self-Publishing endeavor. Did you hire an Editor to revise your work?

I did not, but I joined an editing group and had a few beta readers. I don't regret not hiring an editor, I never could have afforded one, and my work would still be just sitting on my computer, an unedited mess. I have, however, updated my original work since it has been out due to a couple of missed typos. I have a better, more edit-focused plan for my next book.

Was it difficult finding the right cover and blurb?

Cover, no. I found it on a pre-made site and got it relatively cheap, all things considered. All it took was some shopping online. Blurb? I've rewritten it a few times, and I still don't really know if it's good enough.

What made you decide to go the self-publishing route?

I went to an author meet and greet last year and met some great writers. It was a book festival for traditionally published authors and had forums where they would answer questions. One author said that it took them ten years to get published, and they were almost proud of that fact. My only thought was, "This mama doesn't have time to jump through hoops for ten years."

In another forum, a self-published author asked a publisher on the board why he should consider submitting a different work to the traditional route when his first work was fairly successful. The representative hemmed for a while and finally said, "Publishers are more accepting of previous self-published authors than they were five to ten years ago, and libraries rarely buy self-published books." I didn't know much about writing or being an author, but I didn't look at libraries as my target audience. After a friend urging me to give Smashwords a go, this experience was my final push into the Indie world.

Keep up with Emma Woods:

Blog: https://theemmawoods.wordpress.com/
Facebook: https://www.facebook.com/theemmawoods/
Twitter: https://twitter.com/theemmawoods

BOOK
REVIEWS
FOR
WRITERS

- THE MARTIAN

- THE LOST GATE

- SOMETHING STRANGE AND DEADLY

CHAPTER TEN

Learning From Those Who Came Before

The best thing you can do to improve as a writer is to read those who have come before. Of course, reading is good, but reading with the right mindset is even better. Let's take a look at three bestseller novels for what worked and didn't work for them, and what we can learn from it.

The Martian

"**The Martian**" by Andy Weir. Realistic Sci-Fi Thriller.
What writers can learn from reading The Martian: How to incorporate real researching into a novel, how to juggle first and third person point of views, and how to add tension and humor to the story. (It is a thriller, after all.)
There are no spoilers in this review.

My rating (1 to 5 stars): 5 stars!

About the book: A thriller of an astronaut that has been unknowingly left alive on Mars while his crew thinks him dead. He must use his wits and good sense of humor to stay alive long enough to figure out how to get home.

What got me interested into reading this book was not the premise, but rather the way this book has become so popular. I don't normally read anything other than fantasy. It takes a lot for me to read something that is in the realm of realism or Sci-Fi, much less a thriller. This book taught me a lot about how to become successful as a writer, which I will explain in this review along with why I liked the book.

Andy Weir actually had this novel as a series available for free on his website. After getting positive feedback from fans he self-published it in 2011 as an eBook on the cheapest price available: 99 cents. In three short months he sold over 35,000 copies! Just goes to show, good books need a price tag on them. It's that catch 22: if it's free then the audience might think it's not worth having. After all, if it's good enough I'll want to pay for it, right?

By 2014 Weir had finally settled with a literary agent and got hundreds of thousands of dollars for the deal. (Any self-publishing author's dream.)

For Writers: What can you learn from Weir?

What made this book so successful? Well, just reading the first few chapters paints a very clear picture why. Weir did his research, and he did it without holding anything back. I looked into his background, and while he's not a professional engineer or scientist, he's something far beyond that. He's someone that learns all the technical aspects of orbital mechanics and chemistry because he WANTS to. As an engineer myself, I can vouch that while we are trained with a basic understanding of physics, and even I loved the class I took on orbital trajectories, it takes a real passion to learn this stuff without a paycheck at the end of the road. But sometimes karma plays a hand, and Weir got the paycheck he deserved for filling his brain with such beautiful knowledge.

The amount of research alone is what makes the book such an amazing read. And what makes it an INTERESTING read is the marvelous sense of humor he has given the main character: Mark Watney. This book had me laughing from the first sentence. I can find comfort in this poor astronaut's situation of being stranded on Mars with such a good sense of humor. I'm thrilled to see how Hollywood plays this out on the big screen.

Key Points:
Things I liked:

• Unique chapter structure.

Something very interesting about this novel's structure is that it's in a journal format for most of the book. I have no idea how they're going to pull off a movie with this, but it'll be interesting to see how they do! But when we are seeing Watney's struggle, we get a real keen insight into his humor and how he handles things. Around page 49 I was quite startled to realize the story had shifted to a third person point of view, but for the purposes of storytelling I felt it was necessary.

• The sheer amount of realistic physics, math and chemical compositions that were accurate.

I can't imagine how long it took to calculate all the math that went into this novel. I think this is really what made it so successful. It was not easy to do, not everyone can do it, and it makes for a fascinating and realistic reading experience. But I'll admit, a few portions I skipped over because I'm an engineer in real life, too much like my day job! At least for the most part, Weir kept it interesting by including Watney's sense of humor and putting things into Laymen's terms. But he didn't call the reader stupid, and explained everything down to the decimal place and realized we are capable of understanding the concepts if it is explained.

• Great sense of humor for the main character – Watney

This story would not have worked without the character's rough sense of humor. It's necessary for his survival, and it's necessary for the reader to feel the entertainment value of otherwise dry material. Sure, someone getting stranded on Mars is exciting for all of five minutes, then we need something holding up the entertainment value other than worry for Watney. Speaking of which, I was terrified for Watney the whole time and it was well done!

Things I didn't like:

• Some newbie author mistakes were apparent – Third Person PoV Scenes Mostly.

While I liked the third person addition, I could tell that Weir struggled with the prose. It was not as fluid as the journal entry portions. The passages are riddled with unnecessary dialogue tags, adverbs, and general writing no-nos. For example, writing "Suddenly," when just stating the action will be more "sudden" for the reader. But I'm not sure if the regular reader will pick up on this, as an author and a hobby editor I picked up on some of these things.

• A clue that wasn't a clue.

On page 176 of the paperback version there's a chapter break and I think Weir is leaving a cliff-hanger that hints at a future plot point. I don't know if it's intended that at this point the reader can figure out a guess to what may happen, but I had really no clue. I like to think myself fairly proficient to pick up on clues, but there wasn't enough information to let me feel satisfied that I knew what was going on. This made me feel a little frustrated until it was revealed what this clue was all about (100 or so pages later). I would have liked it better if the clue was more obvious, or if it wasn't pointed out at all. Just a personal quibble there.

The Lost Gate

This is a look at "**The Lost Gate**" by Orson Scott Card to see what we can learn from this amazing and experienced sci-fi writer.

My rating (1 to 5 stars): 3 stars ... but I believe it could have easily been 5 with some fixes

About the book: I won't use Amazon's blurb because I think it makes the novel sound terribly boring, so I'll sum it up for you. It's a fantasy written for adults about a teenage boy who lives on a secluded compound filled with Norse gods and magical creatures. At first, you'd think this novel has a whole world on its own away from reality, which it does of course, but the majority is written in good 'ol America. (I wish someone had warned me because I was completely disillusioned when Walmart appeared on my pages.) Once the magic hits however, it's an exciting and fun ride.

What I did like:

1. **Like: World-Building.** The world-building was incredible and vivid. Part of this is because Card borrows from Norse mythology and spends a lot of time in the real world, and you usually can't go wrong with that.

But he does manage to build a unique magic system even through this, centering around of course the "gates." I think I've always been partial to worlds about instant transportation. The idea is fascinating and wonderful, and also frightening for those with such power if they have ill intentions. These are all points Card explores and I enjoyed the musing even when it's dangerous to do so in a novel.

For writers, be sure to have a complex and exciting world for your readers to explore and enjoy. Taking a page from Card, using existing mythology can be a wonderful method to get one foot in the door by using pieces of a world the reader is already familiar with. But don't be afraid to make up your own rules, no matter how similar or dissimilar your world becomes to established myths.

2. **Like: Easy to Read Prose.** I consider prose that enables an author to maintain a voice without being distracting one of the most important elements in a good novel. If I'm constantly distracted by quirky writing, I'm going to have trouble getting into the story. Card does a wonderful job of being just the right amounts of descriptive, colorful, interesting, and maintaining clarity throughout the story.

3. **Like: Humor**. While there's not a ton of humor, Card did fit a few places in there that made me giggle, and it can be a pitfall of fantasy novels not managing to find time for humor. Kudos to Card.

4. **Like: Unique Feature**. A completely mystical world with its own PoV is written alongside the real-world and Danny. It was done well and I enjoyed the variety. It almost felt like I was reading two separate books with the same magic system. (This point is kept vague to avoid spoilers!)

What I didn't like:

1. **Dislike: Lack of Character Development.** I was shocked to realize that the characters, no matter how initially fascinating, never once evolved in this novel. And I think this is likely a result of rushing the novel's final draft. Card is an established author with editors who are already extremely familiar with his work. I can see how it could be easy to let a novel out into the world before it's ready, be it to meet deadlines or by having too much confidence in an author you trust. I'd like to read more of Card's work in this series to see if this is a recurring issue, because everything else in this novel was so well thought-out I was pretty shocked to find the lack of emotional attachment I had with the characters. Given how many awesome other books Card has written, I want to give him the benefit of the doubt and continue the series.

At this point, a typical reader would leave it at "I didn't have emotional connection" and move on to the next book. But I'm going to go a bit deeper to why I felt this way to help you avoid this mistake, because it's easy to avoid if you know it's there, or rather not there! And the simple reason is this, not once did I ever hear what Danny, the main character, the hero, the guy we're supposed to care about, actually wanted. Not a single moment in the entire book did he express his desire for the future, or his fears of why he wasn't going to get it. He complained about the past, and the current issues at hand, but he never actually made a plan for what he was going to do to reach whatever his goals were, which were never revealed, or didn't exist at all.

This is what made me want to stop reading. I wanted to love Danny, but he was an emotionally dull character. I had no reason to care what happened to him because I just couldn't get in his shoes. And while the ending was actually better than I expected, and I read it for the sake of this review, it still didn't answer these questions like I had secretly hoped.

It's a shame because something like this could have been fixed in a revision. All I needed were some self-reflecting moments or clues to what Danny actually wanted, and a fear throughout the novel that he wouldn't get it. Sure, I was afraid for his life, but I needed more than that. Danny himself wasn't all that concerned for his life anyway, so if that was the main motivator it was a poor one.

2. **Dislike: The Title.** It makes no sense given the content of the novel, and feels like the name of the original idea for this novel and it's since been revised. No gates were actually lost, they were stolen. This isn't a spoiler because it's made evident very early in the novel. Even in the very first chapter it goes on and on about how the gates were stolen, and this theme is kept all the way to the end of the novel. I was convinced the name of this novel was "The Gate Thief" and you can imagine my confusion when I went to look up this novel online: "What? The Lost Gate? -- *Checks my book cover* -- When did that happen?!"

I wonder if Card was painted into a corner, because the next novel in this series is actually called "The Gate Thief." Even so, I don't feel like "The Lost Gate" was an appropriate name for this book and is misleading to events that never occurred.

3. **Dislike: Rushed Ending.** When the climax came jogging up like an unwelcome salesman, it felt like the characters were trying to justify to themselves that it was time to cash in and end the story, and they were barely able to convince themselves, much less me, that this ending had come due to the culmination of Danny's choices rather than the author reaching a quota of words and saying "okay I need to stop the story now." And this is not an exaggeration, there is a conversation between the major characters at the end justifying why the end had come and why they couldn't delay it.

Final Comments:

Some may be surprised I only rate this novel 3 stars, but I stick to my guns on this one. The Lost Gate has so much going for it, yet the important stuff got left behind. I didn't care what happened to Danny, and even stopped reading two chapters before the book ended! (Then I decided I wanted to review it, and forced myself to finish it, and somewhat enjoyed it in spite of myself because the world building is amazing.) No matter how awesome other aspects in the book are, the emotional connection needs to be there.

Yet, as a look at this novel with writer goggles, there are some amazing techniques and lessons we can learn. Understandably, for Card is one of the best.

Something Strange and Deadly

Something Strange and Deadly by Susan Dennard A.J. Rating: 4/5 stars. I want to start off by saying this author's work was recommended to me during my search for the "perfect" YA Debut novel. I want to focus on YA writing, so the best way to learn to write is to study those who have come before, and Susan Dennard's work is a great place to start.

I'll start with the spoiler-free book review for those interested in reading it, and I have three main positive comments to discuss.

Book-y Book Review!
1. This is a zombie novel for people who don't like zombie novels.

I know this sounds weird, but it's absolutely true. Just imagine a 16-year-old girl in her fru-fru Victorian era ball gown running around daring to talk to men without a third party introduction, and occasionally swatting at a zombie with her parasol. That's the gist of it (but way better than I make it sound haha).

The zombies aren't the main focus of the novel, though they're the main incentive to get the excitement, and the story, going. They're the constant backdrop that pushes the momentum like a steam train. Without the "Dead," as they're called in this book, there wouldn't be much oomph. But even with that hanging over our heads, the story is focused on the character's personal plight, making the "Dead" just an obstacle she must overcome, and doesn't deviate from her goals for anything. Well, scratch that, it slightly deviates for an enjoyable romance which the main character immediately berates herself for losing focus.

2. The storyline momentum is lovely and linear. It reflects the perfect prose leading us through the story at a comfortable jog.

This novel does an excellent job of having a one-track ride focused on what the main character wants. It's brought up on the first page, and goes all the way to the end. This feels like the main reason this book seems so crisp and clean, and that's because there aren't a bunch of messy or unnecessary side plots to trip us up. We have one clear goal, and we're on a ride to the finish until we get there. I don't know if this is a YA trait, or just a good general rule, but I found myself enjoying its simplicity.

If it weren't for Susan's immaculate and entertaining prose, I don't think the linear aspect of this story would be quite as enjoyable. But needless to say, the prose was perfect, and the storytelling hooked me in every single page. What else is there to say?

3. The romance is done well, but doesn't dominate the novel.

I won't go into this much for the sake of avoiding spoilers, but I appreciate when a novel has a romance that's just an attractive side dish. It's done tastefully and I quite enjoyed how it was executed.

Okay time for dislikes. Not my favorite part of a book review, but it wouldn't be thorough to exclude them just because I liked the book.

1. Politics

The novel itself is so character-intensive that I was thrown off when politics became a heavy issue after the mid-point of the novel. Plot wise, I understood, but I would have been happier without it. I don't mind politics of the completely fantastical nature since I'm not familiar with the world and not attached to it. But I do mind modern politics being discussed and judged in my fru-fru zombie swatting action. Let's just say I skimmed a few pages until it got back to the good stuff.

2. Implausible/Unnecessary Scene

Early in the book a séance is being held as part of the party's entertainment. I accepted that without an issue since it was a popular party gag during the late 1800s. However, out of the party guests, one couple was described as boring our main character with their wish to discuss the preacher's latest sermons. I found that pretty strange. Most churchgoers wouldn't be caught dead going to a séance (pun intended-haha), as it's heavily against the religion and ironically also preached against in sermons.

So at this point, I was expecting to read how this couple was perhaps complaining about the fact there was a séance, or something to explain why this detail was there, but talk of this couple didn't come up again. There is only one sentence that describes this scene, and it's in parentheses, and it could have been left out without changing the story or the scene at all. So I felt it would have made more sense just to not include it, as I was waiting for an explanation why churchgoers would be at a séance for the remainder of the chapter and never got one.

3. I'm in a love/hate relationship with the last chapter

No spoilers, so I won't elaborate more than saying the ending was stellar and managed to surprise me, but at the same time it wrapped up with a "whelp, here are all the things I plan on doing in book 2, READ IT OKAY?" The tone just pulled too much out of the main character dealing with the ending resolutions and already speeding towards the new story threads for book two. I will keep reading, and I didn't need the push and the shove to do it.

That concludes the reader portion of the book review! Keep reading if you are a writer and would like to review my notes for what can be learned from Something Strange and Deadly for writing a YA Fantasy novel.

Warning: SPOILERS AHEAD (Until Page 115)!

Writerly Lessons

1. Keep the plot, as well as the prose, clear and concise. And most importantly, end when the core conflict is resolved.

As I mentioned earlier, the storyline is extremely linear. In any novel, but YA especially, linear storytelling is an important trait. The main issue in Something Strange and Deadly is Eleanor's wish to find her missing brother who has seemingly been kidnapped by the Dead, and that drives all of her actions. It is her main motivator and because it's an honorable goal, we support all her acts of rebellion because she's being completely selfless.

Aside from making the character likable and giving the reader a clear understanding of her motivations, it allows the story to have a clear thread to follow. Each chapter is unraveling the mystery of what's happened to her brother, why, and what she's going to do about it. And when we finally find him, that's when the story concludes to its end, as it should.

What I also notice is how clean Susan's prose is throughout the novel, and there are very few awkward places. There are also very few instances where unnecessary things or instances are described. There's no repetition like some debut novels tend to do. If you don't know what I mean by repetitive, then that means you need to study prose. And no, I don't mean using the same words like "he *step*ped on the *step*" as "repetitive," although that's a no-no as well.

Not to go on a tangent, but this reminds me of one of my favorite quotes:
"If you have any young friends who aspire to become writers the second-greatest favor you can do them is to present them with copies of 'The Elements of Style.' The first-greatest, of course, is to shoot them now, while they're happy." - Dorothy Parker

2. Write to your target audience.

Susan's target audience, if I had to guess, are fantasy readers who enjoy Victorian era/Steampunk-esque stories. We don't typically read zombie novels, and ironically this book is heavily about zombies, but at the same time it's not like any zombie novel you'd see out there. That's because the zombie readers are actually not the target audience.

There are plenty of instances where Victorian era quirks are explored, and I thoroughly enjoyed them. My favorite was when the main character realized she introduced herself to a man without a third party introduction during her early rebellion stages to find out what's happened to her brother.

At the same time, I feel Susan wrote herself into a corner. The main character, Eleanor, constantly lies to her mother where she's going, constantly manages to get a chaperone or invent one, and often has to make excuses. I found it entertaining at first, but then after a while it grew to be a bore and verged on not being believable. With the linear story structure, we can't have side-plots to explore how she manages to do what needs doing to find her brother while disregarding social graces expected of her class. So it winds up being rushed and unclean.

To elaborate, her mother is not an idiot, and should have been able to realize something was up. I would have liked it if there had been a few more scenes where Eleanor had to get more creative to get her mom off her back, or just confronted her about what was actually going on. The mother is painted out to be this selfish woman who almost sees her daughter as property to marry off to bring the family wealth and respect again, and after losing her husband and her son's nowhere to be found, why would she treat her last remaining family member this way? I just found it to be a stretch, and I wanted the mother to be more likable. Even at the end, the mother is just casually mentioned as being holed up in her bedroom and never coming out, and is still resistant to doing anything that may tarnish her family's reputation.

While that issue existed, the target audience was still maintained and I understand why the mother didn't get a character arc. The audience Susan targeted probably didn't care much for the mother, and was fine with this lack of character development. It was a common theme throughout the story that there weren't a bunch of loose ends or unnecessary side plots. We have the main story with its complicated history and anything else that doesn't support this spiderweb doesn't get developed. So in that sense, I understand why the mother is just a plot device. The audience wouldn't have wanted her to have a side character development and conclusion because it didn't support the main theme. It would have just complicated things and given the reader more to worry about.

All-in-all, I enjoyed this book and want more. I'm looking forward to reading the sequel, "A Darkness Strange and Lovely!"

TWITTER
PITCH
CONTESTS

CHAPTER ELEVEN

Twitter Pitch Contests

4 Tips to a Stellar Twitter Pitch

Earlier in this guide I mentioned "4 Tips to a Stellar First Chapter" where I received a Revise/Resubmit request by a publisher. What you may not realize is the reason this publisher and I connected was because I won a Twitter Pitch Contest. The reward of which was a critique of the first three chapters. Awesome, huh? Imagine my surprise when they not only critiqued my chapters, but gave me a Revise/Resub request as well!

I don't want to underestimate the value of participating in these contests. Read on for a review of what a Pitch Contest is, what you can get out of it, and a list of winning Tweets from real pitch contests to see how it's done.

Tip 1: Understand what you're getting into.

What is a Twitter Pitch Contest?

Every few weeks, agents and publishers will host a Twitter Pitch Contest. Terms and rewards will vary, but the basic idea is to give authors a chance to pitch their novels to agents and editors that are otherwise too busy to pay any special attention. The catch is you have 150 characters to catch their eye. If you do, the reward can be otherwise elusive feedback or even landing your agent.

It's hard to stand out in a slush pile, and some may be confused that the "reward" is to submit to the slush pile like everyone else. But think about it, the hardest part of making it out of the slush pile and into the "maybe" pile is getting noticed. If you've already caught their eye, then half the battle is already won.

The most popular pitch contests can be found under these hashtags. Be sure to keep searching for when the next one is going to take place. It only takes a few moments of your time and is worth the effort.

Supported by Pandamoon Publishing:
#PitMad
#AdPit
#pitchmas
#sffpit
#WritePit
Exclusively for Picture Books:
#PBPitch

While these are some of the main ones, keep a lookout for any type of # with pitch in it, since small publishers will also host their own contests here and there. New Pitch contests are popping up all the time, and the easiest way to keep track of these is to follow your favorite agents and publishers. Their notifications will pop up on your feed.

Tip 2: Be prepared! Understand the limitations of the Pitch Contest you will join.

I'll use #PitMad for this example. #PitMad will last for 12 hours, and you are allowed to tweet twice per hour. Meaning you should have 24 pitches ready to go out. If you're not able to set an alarm and send out your prepared tweets on schedule, then try using a free service which allows you to preschedule your tweets. As I don't use these I don't want to recommend any, but feel free to do a google search. I know there are plenty of options out there.

Tip 3: How do I write a Tweet that'll get noticed?

This will be trial and error. You need to find a pitch that works for your novel. And even if you do have a pitch that works, you may still not garner interest from an agent or editor for unknown reasons. (They're looking for someone specific, they didn't check all the pitches, etc.)
So before I go into what I THINK works and what doesn't, here's what worked for me.

Try 1: No Favorites
Azrael is half human, half angel, and forced into a pact with a demon. Who better to prove flaws make us stronger?

Why I don't think it worked:
- There's no interesting twist that sums up why this novel would be interesting. What kind of flaws? Who becomes stronger? And while it's clear who the main character is, it's not clear what's the conflict and goal of the story.

Try 2: No Favorites
The only way left to go from Heaven is down... Azrael, a 16-year-old fallen angel girl will find the strength in her flaws to survive:YA

Why I don't think it worked: While the logline is good, it's too generic and again doesn't grab interest with the bland "strength in flaws in order to survive" idea.

Try 3: Favorite!
What do Angels, a teen girl, and magical tattoos have in common? A life lesson that perfection comes with flaws. Wings not included.

Why I think it worked: The novel has some interesting and unique topics, so why not list them out? That's what I did. And instead of focusing on the theme, I focused on being interesting. "Wings not included" stands out and draws the reader in wondering what that could mean. It's by far the most interesting out of the three I've tried.

In a Twitter Pitch contest, you have to instantly attract the person reading your tweet. If it's confusing, vague or uninteresting you aren't going to have a chance at a favorite. You need to do your best to find what is unique in your novel that can stand out from others. If you say, "Jane must rescue her brother against all odds" I don't think that's going to win a tweet. An agent wants to understand the feel of your novel and what's special about it. Be specific, be interesting, and be fun.

Tip 4: Be ready to win! What do I do if someone favorites my Tweet?

If you're like me, when you do get a favorite you're imagining some other aspiring author liked your pitch and favorited it, even though that's considered poor etiquette. Check the person who sent you a favorite and if they're part of an agency, even if it seems like someone that wasn't tweeting about the event.

Usually the event you've joined will have an originating Tweet which provides a link of how to submit if you win a favorite. Search the #Pitch that you entered under "Top Tweets" and you should find it. This is the best way to make sure you aren't finding some scam link on google. Double and triple check your sources!

Make sure to follow the directions. It's a query like any other and you need to follow the rules. It would be a shame to get this far and be disqualified from review based on deviating from the submission standards.

In your query, be sure to include your Twitter handle so the agent can verify the favorited pitch. It's your chance to stand out from other queries.

Now I'll go through a handful of Twitter Pitch Contests and their winning tweets. For access to the clickable versions of hashtags, publisher and agent Twitter accounts (which I recommend you follow), then download the kindle version of this guide.

Twitter Pitches Galore!

Here starts a long glossary of winning tweets. The purpose of these pages are to show you what works, and to also give you information of what *real* agents and editors are looking for. I've included a large list for the purpose of those looking for a traditional route and may be interested in some of these agencies or publishers. Even if you intend to be self-published, you have even *more* reason to understand pitches. You will have to shoulder the load all on your own to win over readers' hearts, and the best way to do that is to have a killer pitch.

How to use this list:

Each section will focus on one particular pitch contest. I'll explain who is the host and what prizes they are offering. I will then list the winning pitches and who favorited the tweets. This may seem staggering at first and your eyes may want to glaze over, but I encourage you to take the effort to sift through the information. Write down the agents and publishers you find in this list who've favorited tweets with stories similar to yours. Research them. Query them, or wait for the next Twitter Pitch Contest and include their Twitter handle in your pitch. You'd be surprised how often that works. You'll have gotten an edge by doing your homework. Sometimes a foot in the door is all you need.

Glossary:

#PitchCB (Page120) : Curtis Brown Agency. If you're interested in an agency who's been around since 1914, take a look at this section to see the (2) Tweets they favorited, but more interesting, the list of Q & A to try and get in their heads.

#PitchMAS (Page124) : This is a precursor to #PitMad, one of the biggest pitch contests of the year. This list will include a plethora of agents and publishers. Don't forget that you don't *have* to get an agent. If you want to skip the middle-man, it's within your power to do so. There are many large and small publishers who take unsolicited submissions and who also participate in the larger pitch contests.

#PitchBFB (Page 127) : This is an independent pitch contest for an independent publisher. This is meant to illustrate the chance to get amazing feedback. I can personally vouch for this particular contest as I've won twice and I've had 3 chapters of each novel critiqued. I received amazing advice. I encourage you to check out independent publishers for their pitch contests. They will have more time but still have the experience to give you invaluable feedback.

#PitchMatch (Page 130) : This is also a contest run by the same host as #PitMad. This section contains one of the longer lists of agents and publishers and what pitches they were attracted to.

#PitMad (Page 142) : This is the final massive list. The sheer amount of participants are staggering. If you know who you're interested in pursuing, this is a great list to find pitches that caught their interest.

November 2015 #PitchCB

Theme: #DiscoveryDay

#PitchCB : 9AM - 1PM (London Time).
Winning Pitches:

@AlissiaBee; Liked by Curtis Brown Agent: <u>Emma Herdman</u>

Imagine discovering a furnished house in Dulwich. A secret setting for an affair in the 70s. It was abandoned. You need refuge. #PitchCB

@sianushka; Liked by Curtis Brown Agent: Emma Herdman

#PitchCB An academic discovers a woman's memoirs in the G Stein archive. It reveals an extraordinary life at the ❤□ of the 20s Left Bank.

Yes, she used an emoticon heart! Nifty trick to by-pass some word count.

Aside from winning tweets, there was an event which held a discussion of a Sunday Times Top 10 Bestseller author for some Q&A. Here are my favorite tidbits from that event:

#CBBG : 1PM - 2PM (London Time) (Curtis Brown Book Group)
Main topic was the discussion of The Silent Tide, written by Rachel Hore, represented by Curtis Brown. Ironically, the book is about the journey of fictional character Emily Gordon in publishing.

Some favorite Tweets from this discussion:

Q
Van Demal @Van_Demal
#CBBG The title's spot on. Did you know early on that it would be called #TheSilentTide, and hold several meanings? @CBBookGroup @Rachelhore

A
Rachel Hore @Rachelhore
@Van_Demal @CBBookGroup the title came to me about halfway through the book. #cbbg

Q
Emma Herdman @emduddingstone
Had you always wanted to write a book set in the world of publishing? Was it inevitable?! #CBBG #DiscoveryDay

A
Rachel Hore @Rachelhore
@emduddingstone #cbbg Do readers like books set in publishing, do you think?

#CBCTips : 2PM - 3:30PM (London Time)
Also an insightful event. These tweets were Novel Writing Tips from Curtis Brown.

CB Creative @cbcreative

Scenes in novels rarely need to be longer than 1000-1500 words. If yours goes on pages & pages, do some cutting #CBCTips

Don't spend ages introducing characters with their potted life stories before you make things happen to them #CBCTips

Endings don't have to be happy but they should be satisfying - don't just trail away ... #CBCTips

Don't open a novel with a character's hangover, or a bit of bland scenesetting. So so dull ... #CBCTips

Things to avoid: Don't have anyone 'padding' about. Don't have an 'azure' or 'inky-black' or 'cerulean blue' sky. Or crunchy gravel #CBCTips

If you write lots of pounding hearts, unable to breathe etc very early in novel, you leave yourself with nowhere left to go #CBCTips

The end is just the beginning. If you're a real writer, take the rewriting stage seriously. Interrogate your material #CBCTips

Writers get bogged down trying to move characters around. We don't usually need the bus journey there, ringing the door bell etc #CBCTips

#AskCB : 3:30PM - 5PM (London Time)
Some more Q&A from Twitter followers:

Q
Sara D @psychodwarf   (This is actually an editor asking! Shouldn't she know...?)
#askcb ok here's a question...how many authors actually make a living from writing, and how many also have a second 'real' job

A
Gordon Wise @gordonwise
@psychodwarf it's hard to live off your writing; never quit the day job starting out. Figure out a game plan if things start to work #Ask CB

Q
Chloe Esposito @ChloeJEsposito
#AskCB I have a first draft of my novel and am in process of editing. An agent I like is asking to see it ASAP (unedited). Should I send it?

123

A
Jonny Geller @JonnyGeller
@ChloeJEsposito you only get one chance to read something for the first time. Don't waste it!

Q
Kate Todd @KTodd_Writes
In your experience, what types of stories are best served by present tense? What do you think are some of the best examples? Thanks! #AskCB

A
Jonny Geller @JonnyGeller
@KTodd_Writes it used to be a no-no but after Wolf Hall, historical novels have it more and more. It's tough to sustain and can irritate!

Q
Ann Davies @annwritesthings
#ASKCB What are your views on professional editing agencies? Worth the money? Do you give pref to submissions via them?

A1
Richard Pike @LondonFarmBoy
@annwritesthings I wouldn't give preference to submissions from editing agencies, no.

A2
Sophie Lambert @AgentSophieL
@annwritesthings I think that they vary enormously. There are some very good ones and some sharks. I don't give preference to them though

Q
julieP @readmynovels
#AskCB Beta readers and literary consultant say my writing is good, but agents say no thanks with stock replies. Who to go to next

A
Sophie Lambert @AgentSophieL
@readmynovels Keep going I say. It often takes tens of submissions but you *just* need it to click with one person who will champion you

Q
Elaine McCann @ElaineMcCann1
#AskCB How important is it that a new author submitting their work has an online presence/following?

A1
Carrie Plitt @PlittyC
@ElaineMcCann1 it's not necessary - the writing is the most important thing.
But an online following can help

A2
Emma Finn @EmF1nn
@ElaineMcCann1 it's definitely not a priority, especially for fiction. But it can
be a great way to spread word of mouth about your book

A3
Lucy Morris @lucycmorris
@ElaineMcCann1 It's certainly not a hindrance, but the writing's the most
important thing #askCB

A4
Gordon Wise @gordonwise
@ElaineMcCann1 just be prepared to cultivate one later on #AskCB

Usually #PitchCB runs the fourth Friday of every month, but I'm not sure if they'll be running for Christmas. So check in at Curtis Brown's Website for the latest updates on the next Twitter Pitch Contest!

December 2015 #PitchMAS

I'm happy to provide you this tidy list of winning tweets for #PitchMAS!

I am also proud to announce my winning tweets, which drew the attention of 1 agent (Mike Hoogland from DGLM) and 1 publisher (Pandamoon). It was a great opportunity to correspond with Mike Hoogland and gain feedback that while my novel was not his cup of tea, he felt the premise and narrative voice were strong. Invaluable feedback to know whether or not I'm going in the right direction!

AJ Flowers winning tweet:
@AJFlowers86
When you know you'll be reborn, is giving your life really a sacrifice? Ask
Sarah's father, if you can find him before the gods do. #PitchMAS

Other notable tweets (in no particular order):

(All hashtags and twitter handles are clickable)

Fav by 1 publisher (Curiosity Quills Press)
G.L. Morgan@GLMorganAuthor
The Cauldron Bearer is a #retelling of the Welsh folk story "The Spoils of Annwfyn" set in 4th-C Britain #Pitchmas #HF Mists of Avalon+Hild

Fav by 2 publishers (PandaMoon & Samhain Publishing)
Kristi DeMeester@KMDeMeester
Cora, on assignment at a snake handling church, uncovers demonic possession.What wakes is older than the devil. And hungry #PitchMAS #horror

Fav by 1 publisher (REUTS)
Melanie Stanford@MelMStanford
Trevi wants the lead in the musical. Someone wants her heart in a jar. She must uncover the mystery or lose her heart forever. #YA #PitchMAS

Fav by 1 publisher (REUTS)
Maddie Rue@WriteMew
Fighting to survive prison, a 17-yo girl risks escape w/ a borderline sociopath, not expecting love to jeopardize freedom #PitchMAS #SF #YA

Fav by 1 agent (Mansion Street)
Melissa Hed@MelissaHed
When her homecoming crown transfers to her nemesis, dead girl won't RIP til bitch gives back her bling #YA #ghost #comedy #LGBTQ #PitchMAS

Fav by 2 publishers (REUTS & Curiosity Quills Press)
Laura Pohl@laurampohl
In #YA retelling of Ivan and the Firebird, the daughter of death must save her kingdom by finding legendary bird #PitchMAS

Fav by 2 publishers (Boroughs Publishing & Fantasy Works Publishing)
Dana Nuenighoff@DanaNuens
A witch w/ powers she can't control must trust a demon w/ a past he can't escape to rescue her dad's soul. CHARMED + AIRBENDER #PitchMAS #YA

Fav by 1 publisher (REUTS)
Jenny Schoberl@holdin_holden
Is father lying to her? The only way for Anais to find the truth is to break his rules, but defying Death may lead to hers. #PitchMAS #YA

Fav by 2 publishers (Samhain Publishing & SourceBooks)
Heidi Peitz@hpeitz
(DarkAngel+Xmen) Evie must hide powers from military she serves or be weaponized. Handsome fellow soldier vows to protect her. #PitchMas #NA

Fav by 1 publisher (Fantasy Works Pub)
Ninan Tan@NinanTanster
Folklore+mythology lead sick 16yo girl to explore magic in Nepal+Morocco+Romania and more in her dreams STILL ALICE+NARNIA #PitchMas #YA #F

Fav by 1 publisher (2 editors favorited, but both were from Curiosity Quills Press, I guess they liked this one!)
Laura Jardine@authorLJardine
#PitchMAS #R Almost-billionaire/MMA star + plain librarian have fake relationship...in a town full of romance novel characters. #romcom

Fav by 1 publisher (Jolly Fish Press)
Ninan Tan@NinanTanster
16yo girl with neurodegenerative disease explores folklore & mythology around the world as she spirals into dementia. #PitchMas #YA #SFF

Fav by 1 publisher (Jolly Fish Press)
JAHaymanWrites@JAHaymanWrites
The world sleeps but Alex is awake. He can see the injustice, the horrors of this place. He will wake us all. He has to. #SFF #pitchMAS

Fav by 1 publisher (Jolly Fish Press)
Greta Boris@GretaBoris
Gwen, Lance, Art and a deranged murderer meet in Orange County. A killer twist on Camelot. Book 1 of 7 Deadly Sins series. #PitchMAS #A #T

Fav by 1 publisher (BookFish Books)
Claire Andrews@cmandrewslit
Young woman must stop those who want to destroy Olympus before war ignites between men and gods. #PitchMAS #YA #SFF
Fav by 1 publisher (BookFish Books)

Annie May Snowflake@MayWriter
GUARDIANS OF THE GALAXY meets THE MATRIX: Ragtag group of friends travel the galaxy to find a way out of a videogame #PitchMas #Ya #SF #LGBT

--
A.J. Flowers Comments

It was interesting to see the kind of favorites that popped up for #PitchMAS, since it's a contest held very shortly after the other major contests such as #PitMAD and #SFFPit. I feel a lot of authors pitched the same or similar pitches as they did for other contests, since there are different agents who attend per contest. But at the same time, there are going to be many who've participated in all the contests, and this is your second chance at the agents or publishers who weren't interested the first time around.

It's difficult to come up with new pitches for the same novel, trust me I know, but if you can even come up with one good new one, it's a chance to connect and network. In my case, this is what happened for me. It's the third pitch contest I participated in during December and I still connected with someone new and got valuable feedback! Nothing is harder to get in this industry than feedback, and if you participate in these contests for no other reason, at least do it for that.

January 2016 #PitchBFB

I'm happy to announce the winners for the Twitter Pitch Contest #PitchBFB hosted by independent publisher Book Fish Books on January 13th from 7AM - 7PM EST. The rules for this pitch contest were 3 pitches allowed per project, and seeking only MG, YA, and NA novels.

Prizes (Copied from Book Fish Books site):

--If we like your pitch, we promise to offer personalized feedback on your submission!
--Also, a few submissions will receive complete critiques from our content and line editors on the first three chapters of their work.
--And finally, one participant will receive a full critique from our content and line editors on their FULL manuscript!

This section is to provide you a list of the winners so you can study what makes a great Twitter Pitch and how you can get your book in the spotlight in the future. Be sure to check out other Twitter Pitch Contests (listed at the end of this section) and their winners to see what your favorite publishers or agents liked, and get an idea what they're looking for.

Book Fish Books was also nice enough to post what they were looking for before the contest:

Heather Powell @HLVanFleet
You know what I haven't asked for in a while? Sports romances, YA or NA. If you have one today, do #PitchBFB for guaranteed feedback. #MSWL

Erin Rhew Books @ErinRhewBooks
#PitchBFB: What would I like to see?? #Mythology (#YA or #NA), unique #dystopian or flawed utopian, #scifi, non-prince/princess #fantasy.

Now for the winners!

I am pleased to announce my winning tweet for Sanctuary:

Alyssa Flowers @AJFlowers86
Is giving your life really a sacrifice if you know you'll be reborn? Ask Thane, if you can find him before the gods do. #pitchbfb #NA #F
And here are the other wonderful winners, listed in no particular order:

Kirk Kraft @KAKraft
#PitchBFB Jared's best friend might "like" him & his arch-nemesis likes her. He'll lose her forever if he can't figure out what he feels #MG

Anna Mercier @AnnaRMercier
Chasing her father's final steps leads Ada to her new job as a Grim Reaper. But death might be the only way to save her family.#PitchBFB #YA

Carolyn LaRoche @CarolynLaRoche
#NA Cape Cod summer, handsome baseball player, sweetness of new love. Will Mandy take the risk or let her past control her future? #PitchBFB

Cameron Eldridge @cam_eldridge
When Morelle sees a face, she hears a number 1-10, ranking them from good to evil. Now she must prove the mirror wrong. #YA #PitchBFB

Mica Scotti Kole @micascotti
Tyrant Rider sees odd magic in servant K-1, forcing both to uncover their blurred pasts and cruel fates within a dying world. #PitchBFB #NA

Holly Flynn @hollyflynnigan
Under an empire kept strong by fear and submission, a small act of kindness blossoms into love and changes the world. #NA #PitchBFB

Julie Lonewolf @juliethewolf
There are only 2 options: protect vulnerable royal demigod from stalker or die trying. Either way Dom may lose her. #PitchBFB #PNR #WNDB #NA

Julie Lonewolf @juliethewolf
#PitchBFB #NA Demigod w/PTSD. W/help from disabled #milspec sent to protect her, she may learn to forgive herself & love him. #POC #R

AftenBrook Szymanski @aftenbrook
Sixteen-yo Brynn has no time to investigate the murder of a neighbor's toddler, until a voodoo doll hints at her own watery grave #PitchBFB

J. @JL_Dugan
When out/proud Kyle falls for a closeted fb player, both boys realize sometimes you have to risk losing it all to have it all #YA #PitchBFB

Patrick Holloway @PatOHolloway
When a teenage misfit ends a school shooting with bare hands, it places him in a religious conspiracy attempting to kill God #PitchBFB #YA

Sandy Panting @SandraPanting1
Can Brady follow through with putting his yet unborn child up for adoption, and what about his feelings for another girl? #YA #PitchBFB

Renée A. Price @ReneeAPrice
#PitchBFB EMMY&OLIVER meets CATCHING JORDAN when Noah attends a soccer camp in Rio & falls for former BFF, the owner's forbidden dgtr. #YA

Hetal Avanee @HetalWrites
Fake ID & real smarts got Asha to Mumbai; now to infiltrate & dismantle lives of people who decimated her life. #PitchBFB #NA #UF w/#R

Hetal Avanee @HetalWrites
They made her run, made her hide, killed her parents, & took her sister. 22yo Asha's in Mumbai to even the score. #PitchBFB #NA #UF w/#R

Monica M. Hoffman @mmhoffman14
#PitchBFB 17yo fighter pilot Evie kicks ass--but she's only human. After rogue Android saves her cocky ass, nobody but Evie can save his.#SF

Lindsay Kroeger @Lkroeger007
#PitchBFB #NA #F Things are about to get dicey. Empathic twins, a sexy neighbor, a shady girlfriend, and a secret fae lab? Oh, my...

Gayle Clemans @gayleclemans
*Isaac seeks a cure for his Midas touch. Trailed by greedy men, he falls for the girl who helps him. But he must not touch her. #YA **#PitchBFB***

Sara Jo Cluff @SaraJoCluff
*When Cassidy's crush is stolen by her bully, she turns to a 12-step program to win him back and end her bully's time in office **#PitchBFB** #YA*

Jacqueline Dooley @jackie510
*#YA An emotionally scarred dragon & 15yo Mac must work together to stop a disease spreading through Spiritwood's linked worlds. **#PitchBFB***

Jade M Hemming @jadewritesbooks
***#PitchBFB** #SF #YA Sara's duty: alter/correct timelines as instructed. But when her friends are due to be erased it's time to break the rules*

Writerwoman @hannahrgoodman
4 high school friends. 3 secrets. 2 weeks in paradise. 1 huge explosion. Steamy, contemporary NA told from alternating POVs.

#PitchBFB
And that's all the winners! Book Fish Books has their work cut out for them. As a previous winner to this contest who received feedback, I have to pat them on the back. They do a thorough job and don't cut any corners. It's REAL feedback. A big thanks to Book Fish Books for this awesome contest.

February 2016 #PitchMatch

This was certainly a new and fun Twitter Pitch Contest hosted by Brenda Drake, otherwise known for the popular Twitter Pitch Contest, #PitMad. (Click here to read the host's page.)

Their Twitter handle lists this contest as:
A collaboration between #MSWL and #PitMad. Three teams of cupids (writers, agents, editors) compete to make the most literary matches. February 11, 1-4 EST.

Basically, the teams of cupids rummage through the 3 hours of pitches and hold them up against #MSWL (Manuscript Wish List) posts from agents and editors. If they feel they've found a match, they bring the pitch to the agent/editor's attention. If the agent/editor favorites the tweet, that means they are interested and hopefully the cupids have created a love match!

Agents are busy people. Really. Busy. People. Events like these help authors to rise above the slush pile with a little extra oomph, and sometimes agents who aren't even open to submissions will make exceptions if they make a connection through a pitch contest like this one.
And if that isn't enough of a reward for you, then look at it this way. #MSWL got a decent refresher!

First, the winning tweets! Sorted by agent and including their posted #MSWL just to compare how accurate their #MSWL is to their interest in pitches. This isn't just to see the winners, but to better understand agents and publishers, and what it is they're looking for. This is an activity I've done on my own for some time, and I'm an author who is in the spirit of sharing what I learn with others. Writing is not a solo endeavor. We need to stick together!

*Disclaimer:

-This is a listing compiled based on live Twitter feed and is not an official nor complete list since a complete list would take me 1209498456 hours to complete *manic laugh*. There are a TON of tweets, so if I missed yours and you'd like to see it here, feel free to send a comment and I'll add it to the list.

-Additionally, I have no affiliation with this contest. MG and PB are not included.

-If pitches won multiple favorites, they are listed only once.**

Favorited by Literary Agents:

Agent: Mandy Hubbard via Emerald City Agency (She has recently founded her own agency after 6 years with D4EO)
Mandy's MSWL:
#MSWL: *YA where teens fake being adults, a la DON'T TELL MOM THE BABYSITTER'S DEAD.*
#MSWL- *YA with an absurdly ridiculous premise (like KILL THE BOY BAND, or the movie THE HANGOVER.*

Tweets Fav'd by Mandy:
CMM@CMarieMosley
17yo,on the road to redemption & away from home, falls in love w/a girl who holds a secret that could destroy them both. #YA#Cont#PitMatch

Valerie Bodden @ValBodden

#YA#CON Girl popping Adderall while caring for dying mom meets boy pulling risky stunts to prove his life's not a cosmic mistake #PitMatch

Brandy meinhardt @MeinhardtBrandy
He's a burn victim. She chose an abortion at 17. Both carry scars, but together they might heal each other. Dual POV #YA#PitMatch
C J Summerfield @CJSummerfield

Teens face down their emotional & drug-fueled demons at therapeutic boarding school. Some succeed, some struggle and one dies. #PitMatch#YA

Lisa Kogut @Lisakogut3218
As Lauryn fights to survive after a pandemic, she falls for a soldier, helping her forget her dead boyfriend.Until he shows up #pitmatch#ya

J. @JL_Dugan
When out/proud Kyle falls for a closeted fb player, both boys realize sometimes you have to risk losing it all to have it all #YA #PitMatch

Agent: Peter Knapp via New Leaf Literary
Peter's MSWL:
#mswl - smart general fiction for adults. Think ME BEFORE YOU, THE LANGUAGE OF FLOWERS, TO BE SUNG UNDERWATER, THE AGE OF MIRACLES
Tweets Fav'd by Peter:

Lissa Carlino@EWallerCarlino
Eden & Samuel become fast friends. Through abuse, careers, infidelity, & even death, the two never lose sight of their bond #wf#PitMatch

Amanda Lang @FinalGrrrl333
It was just a movie. The ritual sacrifice wasn't supposed to be real. I Know What You Did Last Summer meets The Craft. #PitMatch#YA

Ty Martin @restlesoul
Diary of a Wimpy Kid meets The Martian #LGBT #MG #SF After Earth destroyed, Gilly documents struggle as last surviving human #PitMatch

Agent: Diedre Knight via The Knight Agency

Diedre's MSWL:
I would love to find a Gilded Age novel. #MSWL
I would love to find historical fiction about ancient Sparta, Ancient Greece or Romo. #mswl

133

Tweets Fav'd by Diedre:

Sara-Marissa@SeeSaraScribe

2 save her ppl, Āmitis plays both sides of the war. Falling 4 the Persian King, Cyrus, jeopardizes their lives & 2 empires #ya#hf#f#PitMatch

Ruth Kaufman @RuthKaufman Feb 11

She learns be careful what you wish for when her Chicago acting career & feelings for a hot movie director skyrocket. #RomCom #PitMatch

Agent: Mike Hoogland via DGLM
Mike's MSWL:

Looking for some thought-provoking speculative fiction grounded in realism #mswl

Would love to see some #A #S #T #LF #MSWL #PitMatch. I also wouldn't say no to some #WF and #SF

Tweet's Fav'd by Mike:

Ann Bell Feinstein@AnnBFeinstein

Kate must escape the mob & outwit terrorists to save thousands from VX, the worlds most deadly chemical weapon. #PitMatch#A#T

Philip Ray @ShinobiJedi42

A diverse crew of space nerds hunt down an ancient piece of alien technology with mysterious power. #A#SF#PitMatch

Ann Bell Feinstein @AnnBFeinstein

Kate must escape the mob & outwit terrorists to save thousands from VX, the worlds most deadly chemical weapon. #PitMatch#A#T

Vera Kurian @vera_kurian

ZERO DARK THIRTY meets BEFORE SUNRISE when a mild-mannered Navy SEAL falls 4 a brilliant physicist he frees from captivity #PitMatch #LF #A

Agent: Caitlin McDonald via DMLA
Caitlin's MSWL:

I feel like this goes w/o saying but I'm really really dying for non-Western fantasy. Either on Earth or a secondary-world is fine. #MSWL

BTW, I also handle nonfiction, so hit me up with any particularly geeky book proposals you might have! #MSWL
Also looking for stories set in unusual or remote locations. Could be SFF or contemporary, but stays in the region, not transitory. #MSWL

Also still looking for that Leverage book, you guys! Heists heists heists, please send me your heists! Ideally w/ lots of women #MSWL

Canon bisexuality, for example, I am definitely eager to see more of in media #MSWL

I'd also love books that focus on female friendships--either contemporary or genre fiction. All-female fantasy quest! Girl heist team! #MSWL

I'd love diverse representation that is not presented as "issue books"--just queer, POC, & differently-abled people doing stuff. #MSWL

Big #MSWL day on Twitter today! #1 on my wishlist is lesbians: send me lesbians doing literally anything, I am dying for representation!

Tweets Fav'd by Caitlin:
Kyle W. Kerr@KyleWKerr
#PitMatch Gossip Girl with a twist: Eight gay teens + One secret society + One wild night = One hell of an initiation. #YA#LGBT

London Skye @londonskye007
2099: In a submerged world, 16yo Brit Leila must win a perilous sub race & the ultimate prize: her innocent Papa's freedom #PitMatch#YA#SF

Carleen Karanovic @Carleree
JOY LUCK CLUB/TRISTAN&ISOLDE Epic #YA #HF romance–2 reincarnating lovers split by spell gone wrong. Killer set on dividing them #PitMatch

Agent: Amelia Appel via Micintosh & Otis

Amelia's MSWL:
Last one for now: poignant boy-girl FRIENDSHIP. Not everything has to end in romance. Not everything should. #MSWL

Huge fan of anti-heroes. There has to be something likeable about them, but entirely redeemable..? #MSWL

Literary fiction with oh-so-casual magical realism. Like THE PALE KING, where someone can hover above his desk and it's nbd. #MSWL

Tweets Fav'd by Amelia:
Clare@lcoastrhand
The island has secrets. Isla must know the truth so she can let her dead twin go. He'll do anything to stop her. #pitmatch#a#lf#wf#mr

Lindsay Kroeger@Lkroeger007
After her parents die, empathic Sorrel gains a stalker, her twin becomes distant,BFF goes MIA things get out of hand altPOV #pitMatch #NA #F

Agent: Shira Hoffman via Micintosh & Otis
Shira's MSWL:
The Saddle Club for the next (tech) generation. Frienship and ponies. Need I say more? #mswl

American memoir that explores an unknown story or a hidden facet of history. Killer voice is a must. Think Rocket Boys #MSWL

Contemporary romance for teens with a touch of humor in the vein of @SimoneElkeles Humorous adult contemporary romanc also a win! #R #MSWL

Tweets Fav'd by Shira:
Laura Pohl@laurampohl
GRISHA meets GRACELING in a twisted and dark retelling of classic Russian fairytale "Ivan and the Firebird" #YA#F#PitMatch

K.T. Hanna @KTHanna
Wendy helps orphans become Lost Boys, only to find out Neverland might be more dangerous than London #PitMatch#YA#Retelling#Twist

Sara-Marissa @SeeSaraScribe
#PitMatch#ya#retelling Hook didn't always have 1 hand & she wasn't enemies w/Peter. Jas fell in love w/TigerLily & it tore Neverland apart

Mel Melcer @word_dust
Starbound is Titanic in space with teenagers—and one of them is responsible for the iceberg. Adventure/disaster/romance #PitMatch#YA#SF

Daphne Dubois @Daphne_Dubois
A jilted bride sworn off love.A struggling hockey player desperate for a good luck charm.And the one night that changes it all. #PitMatch#R

Agent: Christa Heschke via Micintosh & Otis

Christa's MSWL:
Beautiful literary #MG or #YA that gives me the feels! #MSWL

Dark, eerie and creepy #YA or #MG. Weird small town mystery. #MSWL

A #YA with a forbidden romance! I have a weakness for these! #MSWL

#PB #MG #YA set in an exotic or unique location (i.e the jungle, mountains of Nepal, Morocco, Thailand etc. etc.) #MSWL

A #YA or #MG with unqiue storytelling sturctures (i.e letters, drawings, unreliable narrator) Think Chopsticks or Why We Broke Up #MSWL

Tweets Fav'd by Christa:
Amber K Bryant@amberkbryant
Nolan must decide whether his love for Clara is worth crossing into a parallel realm that may never let him return home. #PitMatch#YA#SF

Kit Frick@kitfrick
#PitMatch Unreliable narrator w/ a dark secret: Ellory can't forget the fire, fall, blood. But she's not talking. Nonlinear #YA #CON #S

Agent: Shannon E. Powers via Mcintosh & Otis

Shannon's MSWL:

A fun, lighter romance with a lot of quirk and deadpan humor. I loved THE FUTURE FOR CURIOUS PEOPLE by Gregory Sherl. #Mswl

Mysteries with long-buried secrets. Dig them up and let the chaos ensue. #mswl

A YA about friends who do fun projects/challenges/pacts together. Kinda like THE NIGHT WE SAID YES by @laurengibaldi #mswl

Anything with a strong sense of nostalgia. I love characters who have nostalgia for their homes/each other. #mswl

On the lighter side - a YA road trip with a cool, specific premise. There are tons out there so you gotta stand out! Humor a plus. #mswl

A favorite theme: boredom/restlessness leading to trouble. Also love the troublemaker/exasperated type-A friendship combo :D #mswl

I'm a sucker for dangerous girls. But they need to be smart and have real, tangible motives, just like the boys do #mswl

I love moments when characters look at each other thinking "What have we done?" Think THE SECRET HISTORY. #mswl

Tweets Fav'd by Shannon:

Léonie Kelsall@leehotline

UNBROKEN+THE BODYGUARD Kidnapped in Australian Outback, teacher Kayla can pray for rescue–or fight to save her students #pitmatch#RS#A

Jim Ormonde@jimormonde
Every language has a word for soul. What's inside was never in doubt. Until Bernstein's hunt for proof found an enemy within #PitMatch#A#T

Jocelyn E Frentz@Joce_elizabethh
Born with her ancestors' memories, she's the weapon the rebels will kill for, and the girl one soldier will die for. #PitMatch #YA #F

Agent: Alex Barba via Inklings Literary

Alex's MSWL:

MG/YA historical fiction à la the old American Girl book series! Felicity, Kirsten, Addie, Samantha, Molly ... #MSWL
YA where witches are the protagonists #MSWL
YA character-driven boy voice #MSWL

Clean teen YA about that awkward teen phase #MSWL

Fav'd by Alex:
Nicole Lynn Hoefs@nicolelynnhoefs
Sydney's cheating dad & absent mother is all the drama she needs. Insert hot skateboarder & now she's twitterpated. Great. #PitMatch#YA#CR

Dana Nuenighoff@DanaNuens
Dressed as a boy, Val joins an enemy crew to find her kidnapped brother & stop a war, not fall for the captain. 12TH NIGHT #PitMatch#YA#F

Nicole Lynn Hoefs@nicolelynnhoefs
Sydney's cheating dad & absent mother is all the drama she needs. Insert hot skateboarder & now she's twitterpated. Great. #PitMatch#YA#CR

Agent: Kelly via Corvisiero Literary Agency

Kelly's MSWL:
I'd love a dark/gritty high fantasy. Strong female MC, w/ diversity + powerful friendships. Wit, humor, and heroine who saves herself. #MSWL

Tweets Fav'd by Kelly:
The Memory Letters@memoryletters
Yrs ago the Void consumed the colors of the world. Now a brash girl+shy boy must work together to stop its growing darkness #PitMatch#F#YA

Dana Nuenighoff @DanaNuens Feb 11
Dressed as a boy, Val joins an enemy crew to find her kidnapped brother & stop a war, not fall for the captain. 12TH NIGHT #PitMatch#YA#F

Agent: Lisa Abellera via KC&A Literary Agency
Lisa's MSWL:
2nd gen immigrant character, family issues & cultural clashes, navigating both worlds, sense of place/culture #diversity#YA#NA or #A#MSWL |

Contemp #MG or #YA w/fantasy aspects, character discovers/gains special ability but loses it & must deal w/being in world without it #MSWL

Epic sci-fi w/environmental (not dystopian), metaphysical or fantasy aspects. Dune but without the worm. #A #SF #MSWL

Tweets Fav'd by Lisa:
Natasha Razi@swingingstorm
Mysterious curse wipes out family of spell-sellers. Lone survivor blackmails broke, trans thief into finding out why. #Pitmatch#YA#F#LGBT

Agent: Brooks Sherman via The Bent Agency (closed to queries, but made an exception for #PitMatch!)

Brooks's MSWL:
Seeking #fantasy in ALL age categories w/ vivid world-building. Think Chronicles of Prydain, Lockwood & Co., Jonathan Strange... #MSWL

A #YA project that makes me feel like DOPE did. https://www.youtube.com/watch?v=strEm9amZuo ... #MSWL

A #MG or #YA project that touches on the experience of undocumented immigration in the USA. #MSWL

Tweets Fav'd by Brooks:
Joseph Quackenboss@JQuack86
For two millennia, Iblis has awaited his revenge. Can two brothers confront a dark God and still maintain their humanity? #PitMatch#A#F

Agent: Jennifer from Liza Dawson Associates

Jennifer's MSWL:
Funny, maybe slightly quirky #CON #R with a great voice. #MSWL

Quirky specifics: #WF #YA #T #MG or #R that features ballet, food, antiques, art, classic movies, debate, football, Austin, theater. #MSWL

Contemporary realistic #YA with a strong voice that stays away from melodrama. (Loves: Nina LaCour, Stephanie Perkins.) #MSWL

Still yearning for a dark and twisty psychologically driven mystery/thriller. #MSWL #A #T #S #M

Tweets Fav'd by Jennifer:
Natasha Neagle@natneagle
Raine's the sole survivor of The Sweet 16 Massacre. As conflicting memories surface, she realizes everyone lied-even her. #pitmatch#YA#T

Agent: Kurestin Armada via PS Literary
Kurestin's MSWL:
#MSWL Fantasy (urban or otherwise) dealing with the diaspora of a magical community
#MSWL I love characters that are willing to get their hands dirty to reach their goal, that are sly and cunning and ruthless
#MSWL Still into retellings of fairy-tales and myths, but with some kind of twist. Different ending? Gender swapped? You tell me!
See Kurestin's Feed for More...

Tweets Fav'd by Kurestin:

Laura Pohl@laurampohl
GRISHA meets GRACELING in a twisted and dark retelling of classic Russian fairytale "Ivan and the Firebird" #YA#F#PitMatch

Jane Fox@_flyingcrowbar
A Faustian deal unites an African princess and a merman. His soul is damned; her soul is leverage. THE LITTLE MERMAID redux #YA#F#PitMatch

Agent: Mary Moore via K.C. Associates
Mary's MSWL:
Cryptozoologist adventure caper, real world or fantasy world. Lots of monsters. Humorous. #MSWL#SF#F#A or #YA

SciFi about human evolution set in near or far future a la Greg Bear's DARWIN'S RADIO. Strong character development. #MSWL#A or #YA#SF

Historical fiction about ballet set in NYC, Russia, or France. Preferably written by a dancer (pro or amateur). #MSWL#A or #YA#HF

Historical set in San Francisco during the Gold Rush. Rich setting and diverse cast. #MSWL #A #HF

Tweets Fav'd by Mary:
Nancy Rubin Stuart@newestwords
#PitMatch A Hollywood dancing star is romanced by the secretly dying George Gershwin. Her Broadway comeback inspires modern jazz dancing.

Frankie Ash @_FrankieAsh Feb 11
16yo must choose btwn treason & hope when a rebellion ensues aboard her starship. It's Starfleet Academy meets King Joffrey. #PitMatch#YA

Monissa Whiteley @monissa
Australia 1840: To save his selkie friend, Davie has to take on prison authorities, demon hunters and his self-doubt #pitmatch#YA#F

Suzanne Samin @suzannesamin
In a world where they are seen as subhuman, Rhea must harness divine & political power to end her tribe's enslavement. #A#F#LGBT#PitMatch

Anna Frost @Frostanity
After years of crossdressing, K goes to war to "become a man." Instead, he befriends an enemy golem. Japan steampunk. #F#YA#LGBT#PitMatch

Ali Herring @HerringAli
Based on Egyptian mythology, Gil must follow Ra's clues to an ancient artifact before his world and his father are lost #YA#SF#PitMatch

Laura Pohl @laurampohl
GRISHA meets GRACELING in a twisted and dark retelling of classic Russian fairytale "Ivan and the Firebird" #YA#F#PitMatch

Seana Kelly @SeanaKellyRW
Boston construction worker goes back to college and falls for her hot professor. Secret meetings +social media =trouble. #PitMatch #Contemp

Favorited by Publishers:

Curiosity Quills Press
Chess Kendle@ChessKendle
GREY'S ANATOMY+THE ROYAL WE: A surgeon can forgive Prince Cheating—and her sister—or get cabin fever with her lumbersexy ex. #PitMatch#A#R

Reuts Publishing
Dani Donegan@A_ChristineD
When gamer Sunny buys a used laptop, a demonic virus on the hard drive
has a game too: spread The Zer0 Maker, or die #YA#H#LGBTQ#PitMatch

Angela@Freepaperclips
When the Soul Stealer threatens to take stars, Esther must kill souls she's
bound to protect or lose control of the earth. #Pitmatch#YA#F

Lana Pattinson@lana_pattinson
17yo girl shipwrecked in Scotland fights Laird & Selkie to get home but her
rescuer steals her heart GREAT&TERRIBLE BEAUTY #HR#YA#PitMatch

-- *This one almost got a favorite from Agent Mandy Hubbard, but she said
she's not a Selkie fan*

Jolly Fish Press
erin augustine@thepocketqueen
House of Cards+Macbeth.POTUS is LBJ's fate.He doesn't want JFK dead,but
the bastard oilmen LBJ owes won't let 'em both live #PitMatch #A #HF

A.J. Comments:
Like I said before, this is by no means a complete list, as the amount of
action for this contest was massive. And I think you'll agree you've seen
enough as it is. I had so much fun compiling it though and I learned a lot
about my favorite agents and editors in the process.

I hope it helps you to better understand what agents and editors are looking
for. Generally, the pitches matched pretty well with their MSWL. And if any
trends can be noted, it's the typical "YA is hot" and "magical realism" where
one MSWL even asked for "Dune without the Worm" haha. I can't imagine
what's attractive about that but okay. Oh, and let's not forget the MSWL
asking for "lesbians doing anything." I have nothing against lesbians, but I'm
sorry, that's not the sole trademark of a bestseller. But, gotta give the people
what they want, right? (I feel like I should make a Wattpad reference here.
But I'll restrain myself.

March 2016 #PitMad

#Pitmad is always a plethora of pitches, agents, and editors. And as such, the best opportunity to see a live picture of what agents and editors are looking for NOW!

For an overview of #Pitmad, please visit the host blog: http://www.brenda-drake.com/pitmad/

Run Down:

Basic rules are (3) pitches allowed per project and the contest runs for 12 hours from 8AM EST to 8PM EST on the day of the event. The polite rules are only agents and editors should favorite tweets and no one else should favorite or retweet. The #Pitmad feed is clogged enough as it is! Plus getting a favorite from a fan is nice, but kind of a let down at the same time if you thought it was an editor or agent!

If your tweet wins a favorite, this means that agent or editor is interested in your work and would like you to query them. Be sure to research before submitting that you are comfortable with the agency or press which has expressed interest (you don't have to query) and look for tweets from the person who favorited you for submission instructions. There might be a special prize of critique or feedback, and if not you get a special boost above the slushpile by being able to show in your submission that your pitch already caught their eye. The agent or editor will be inclined to already have a positive outlook on your submission, and that's golden!

Disclaimer: Below are a list of winning tweets, and are in no way an official or complete list. PB and MG are not included since that is not a focus of this book. If a tweet was favorited multiple times, it is only shown once in this list. #Pitmad is enormous, so I've only grabbed a handfull of tweets to analyze here.

Here we go!
My winning tweet favorited by Curiosity Quills Press and Kelly (CorvisieroLit). Happy and humbled!

Alyssa Flowers@AJFlowers86
To hell with suitors! Azrael sets her sights on becoming Queen and redeeming fallen angels. If only they were worth saving. #ya #F #pitmad

Agents:

Rebecca Strauss; Literary agent at DeFiore and Co.
Sheldon Higdon@sheldonhigdon
After the unexpected suicide of his father, Prof. Benjamin Cole discovers dark family secrets on the farm he was bequeathed #PitMad#T#S#A
Note: This one got 3 agents and 1 editor favs
Gabe McClure@gabemcclure
#PitMad #YA #SF #R DEADPOOL+WHITE COLLAR+FIGHT CLUB. Infamous antihero&cult leader, Miranda, gets caught by the enemy...then falls for him.

Alec Shane; Literary Agent at Writers House, LLC.
matt the radar tech.@alicecirvin
The Cape- a town of murderous shadows. Audrey escaped 8 months ago. To protect her friends, she'll head back into the fog. #PitMad #A #P

Margaret Bail; Agent at Inklings Literary Agency.
CH Lamb@merrcherr
#PitMad bored to death 20so Milly finds new purpose after a sudden death in the family transforms her from cubicle zombie to newbie PI #A

Elizabeth Keysian@EKeysian
A priceless figurine makes enemies of a Regency widow and the Duke who wants to marry her ward- but then she sees him naked. #PitMad #HR #A

Vanessa Marie Robins; Corvisiero Literary Agent Apprentice
Rachel Lenzi@lenziwrites
Elisabeth jumps into the ocean ... and survives. Now, she has to take inventory of the last four tumultuous years. #PitMad#NA#WF

Saritza Hernandez; Sr. Agent, Corvisiero Literary Agency.
Lynn Forrest@LynnMForrest
When the only good monster is a dead one, she must prove her worth to her best friend before her family kills them both.#PitMad #A #UF #LGBT

Mary C. Moore; Literary Agent at @K_C_Associates,
SquidWords@donttakeSamira
A haughty shaman is ripped from her world to the world of spirits she oppressed. If Vegeta were Alice in Wonderland #pitmad#a#f#irmc#mr

Candace Osmond@candaceosmond
Eternal partygoer, Amy has one night stand w/hot guy. She falls and gets attached only to discover he's a single dad. **#Romance#PitMad**

Allison Hantschel@Athenae
Notorious pirate Anne Bonny is said to have died in prison, or disappeared on the seas. The truth is much stranger: She went home. **#PitMad**

Pande Literary; Boutique literary agency
Rachel Cardel@RachelCardel
Only 9 out of thousands have survived OracleTech's Labyrinth. But Bronwyn must win for a secret cure before her family dies. **#PitMad#YA#SF**

Katrina DeLallo@KatrinaDeLallo
Magic is dying. To save it, a 16yo boy must face death to compete in a trial to become the new guardian and renewer of magic. **#PitMad#YA#F**
Christian Smith@CHSmithAuthor
He never believed in ghosts until the day he died.Now dark spirits seek Gavin's heart to free their master, Will he survive? **#YA#F#PitMad**

Emily Beth Shore@EmilyBethShore
#pitmad#YA DOLLHOUSE + GLASS ARROW - 16yo Serenity is sold to the Menagerie, a Red Light District-style Museum where girls become live art

Allister Nelson@avnelson92
#PitMad#PB A LBGQT Norwegian myth retelling where a brave girl rescues a princess-turned-dragon. Wise witches, adventure, and love abound.

Jen Redmile@JenRedmile
Can a ghost, a Guardian Angel, and their 'alive' friends defeat the school's poltergeist. And if they do, at what cost? **#PitMad#YA#PNR**

Jessika Fleck@jessikafleck
#PitMad#YA#F Naya escapes jail to prove her innocence. Not an easy task: she's mute, has 5 days, & is in love with the guard on her trail.

Katie Garner@garner_kate
A poor fortune teller & a prince in disguise race to decipher a book before the evil inside its pages destroys their world. **#YA #F #PitMad**

Kristy Hunter; Submissions Coordinator & Associate Agent @KnightAgency
Megan Clemons@MeganClemons555
UNDER THE TUSCAN SUN + WE BOUGHT A ZOO Italian widower hires American barista. Can they save caffè & uncover his child's secret? **#WF#pitmad**

Jamie Adams@Jamie_Adams22
Before the revolution is over, Marguerite will kiss a boy and kill a boy. The problem is, she loves them both. #Pitmad#YA alt hist
ARCannon@FanNotions

#YA Alt-hist Marie Antoinette-She doesn't know who to trust at Versailles w/ an assassin and a flirty princess after her new husband #PitMad

Lisa Abellera; Literary agent at @K_C_Associates
Gillian Daniels@gilldaniels
Puck, jester to Oberon, has been exiled from Faerie. Now he's bound to the will of a young woman because she saved his life. #PitMad#YA#F

WightCrow@WightCrow
Govt is chasing her, her love is lying to her, & someone wants to put a chip in her head. Life just got interesting for Mer York #PitMad #NA

Whitley Abell; Literary Agent with Inklings Literary Agency
Jenna Lehne@raddestgirlever
CABIN IN THE WOODS meets TEN. Murphy and co. are stranded at a lake house. Their fears start to kill them off, one by one #PitMad#YA#H

Sharon Pelletier; Lit agent at @dglm
Ruth@rteichro
#PitMad Digging into death of college student/homelessness/corrupt cops? Check. A reporter with secrets of her own? Trouble. #A#M

Lauren Abramo; VP, Literary Agent, & Rights Director at@DGLM
Jennifer R McMahon@BohermoreSeries
#pitmad#ya#mr Maeve ditches college for Ireland to track a dream-haunting, lethal pirate queen & end the centuries-old curse on her clan.

SCBoesger@SCBoesger
Autistic 12 yo boy runs away after finding out dad is not his bio father, and must learn to accept love is more than biology. #PitMad #A

Lindsay Mealing; Assistant to @MandyHubbard at Emerald City Literary Agency
Emily Pichardo@EpicEmP
In a world of fairy tales turned evil, Quinn's hunt to find her family has her joining the Rebels in a magical civil war. #PitMad #YA #F

Publishers:

Entangled Publishing
Rebecca Paula@BeckaPaula
Royal places an ad for a wife in the newspaper as a prank on his older brother, but he's the one about to be fooled. **#PitMad#A#HisRom**

Chelly Pike@ChellyPike
#PitMad#A In Faery truth is the law. Deception's an art. Seduced by 1 brother, captured by the other, Quinn's escape will cost a life.**#F#R**

Harlequin Books
SusanJPOwens@SusanJPOwens
#PitMad#CR#RS Branded as a rogue agent, he attempts to clear his name while saving a feisty journalist who is eager to turn him in.

Literary Wanderlust
Dave.Walbridge@AdviceIShouldHa
I'll dust when I'm dead - he glorious life of clutter. The joy of having plenty of stuff and not stressing over it **#pitmad#humor**
Sealey Andrews@Sealey_Andrews

Seattle: Secondhand store owner must repair her holey past to keep her hand-me-down soul from the demon it once belonged to. **#A#UF#PitMad**

Julie Freyou@juliefreyou
Claire's last chance to understand and get to know her mom are in a series of letters to the people her mom left behind. **#pitmad #wf**

BookFish Books
Maddie Gudenkauf@Maddness22
Sadie isn't a superhero, but she must become one to save her superhero boyfriend and the city he's supposed to protect. **#PitMad#SF#R#YA**

Melissa Veres@melissaveres
Marley wakes up on a cold beach with blood-stained hands, her twin sister's severed arm, and no memory of how she got there. **#PitMad #YA**

Kristy Westaway@KristyWestaway
Hades kidnaps his dream girl, forcing the world into a deadly Winter as the girls' goddess mother hunts them down. **#PitMad#YA#AD**

Andrew Munz@AndrewMunz
A stubborn horse wrangler teams up with a hawk-toating cowgirl to take down a corrupt mayor in this Robin Hood retelling. **#YA#W#pitmad**

Megan Easley-Walsh@MEasleyWalsh

#Pitmad#NA For her he'd go to the end of the world When she disappears, he might have to Romeo & Juliet retold in the American Revolution

Juliet Lyons@WriterJLyons
#PitMad#YA Teen angst and a sexy ghost in the East Wing. Falling in love is never easy...

Tosha Sumner@tlwrites
Track star Callie won't date cyclists. But when she's sidelined by injury, pro-cyclist Trent's the perfect distraction. #PitMad #YA #Sports

eTreasures Publishing
Avril Tremayne@AvrilTremayne
Her friend wants him. Her brother hates him. He needs her. She just wants to use him to catch the man of her dreams. #R#PitMad

Curiosity Quills
Richard Agemo@RichardAgemo
In 16th century London, Queen Elizabeth's old flame—Edward de Vere aka Shakespeare—is tried for treason after staging Hamlet.#PitMad#A#HF

Stephanie Lynn Smith@slsmithauthor
Eden's fight for Miss Universe could win her a crown - or destroy a galaxy on the brink of war. CINDER + RED QUEEN. #YA#pitmad

Jolly Fish Press
Kelley Griffin@AuthorKTGriffin
Falling for your Mob-linked protector could be reckless, especially when his loyalty isn't clear and his boss wants you dead. #PitMad#A#RS

That concludes the list! Now, there were plenty of more winners, and only a selection are listed here to analyze agents and editors current interests. I encourage you to take a look at your favorite agents or editors, and see what they liked, and try to understand why. This will go a long way in finding the right place for your book.

Trends:

• Format

A Tweet will only get a favorite if it is precise. Stakes cannot be vague; it can't be about "the main character must do this or die" it has to be something original and interesting. The format of the tweets seem to be *"Main Character Profession must Blank or Consequences."* This format can be anything.

"Underage gambler must grow a beard or lose his only chance at counting cards... and paying his mom's medical bills." See? Just made that up on the spot. Try to fill in the blanks with your own novel if you find you're not getting attention and give it a try.

• Book Comparisons

Having comparisons weren't in as many winning tweets as I've seen in previous contests. I think the only time including comps is a good idea is if it's matching with the current market and also is an accurate representation of your book. It can be dangerous to give the wrong expectation!

• Alternate History

Pretty much any tweet that included alternate history won a favorite. I think this is either a growing trend, or one of those unique baubles agents love to play with. Historical Fiction is hot right now, so I think Alternate History will be hot as well. It sure sounds fun to write too.

Conclusion

This concludes "A Guide for Writing Your First Novel!" I hope you've been able to recognize pitfalls in your own writing and how you approach this industry. There are a hundred routes to publishing heaven, and some may work better for others. Regardless, doing your research and being prepared, and most of all: learning from those who've already made common mistakes, will help you to meet your writing goals. I wish you all the best, and happy writing!

ABOUT THE AUTHOR

A.J. FLOWERS

THANK YOU
FOR READING!

About the Author

A.J. Flowers is a Book Blogger and Fantasy Author. You can follow her blog at https://ajflowers.wordpress.com. Originally from an island about a mile and a half wide named Sugarloaf key, A.J. discovered new lands and culture through books. Life has drastically changed since her childhood, and she currently resides in Detroit, Michigan as an Automotive Body Designer, which has given her the opportunity to travel the world and experience regions and cultures that she incorporates into her work. During her free time, she saves the world from annihilation on her favorite video games side-by-side with her Dutch husband and princess Blue Russian kitty named Mina.

CPSIA information can be obtained
at www.ICGtesting.com
Printed in the USA
FSOW03n1246171217
42536FS